Train the Dog in Front of You

by Denise Fenzi

First published in 2016 by:

Fenzi Dog Sports Academy Publishing

Copyright © 2016 Denise Fenzi

All uncredited photos © 2016 Denise Fenzi

Designed by: Rebeccah Aube | www.pawsink.com
Paws & Ink! A Creative Blend of Dog Training & Graphic Design

Cover Photo: Brent Grebinoski featuring Jennifer Grebinoski & Moe

ISBN NUMBER: 978-0-9887818-8-7

Table of Contents

Acknowledgements

This book is for those dogs who did not read the "how to" books. Those dogs who made me stutter with surprise, laugh out loud at their lack of cooperation, or cry inside for their obvious distress.

This book is for those dogs who made it obvious that one size does not, indeed, fit all.

This book is for those dogs who made me rethink everything I'd ever said, thought, or read about dogs or dog training.

This book is for those dogs who forced me to acknowledge the need for constant reconsideration of comfortably held truths.

This book is for those dogs who made me swallow my fear of failure, take a deep breath, and dig a little deeper for a new, heretofore untried direction.

This book is for those dogs who I have been unable to reach in the past, and those who I will be unable to reach in the future - the ones who keep me awake at night, distressed and searching for the answer to yet another dog training puzzle.

This book is also an apology to those early dogs I failed miserably to understand, the ones I mistreated out of ignorance, and the ones who bore the brunt of my misdirected anger.

As a result of every difficult dog who has crossed my path, I am a better dog trainer, a better problem solver, and frankly, a better person.

I owe you so much. You have my gratitude.

About the author

Denise Fenzi is a professional dog trainer who specializes in building cooperation and extreme working precision in competitive dog sports teams. Her personal passions are competitive obedience and spreading high quality information about no force (motivational) dog training. In addition to traveling worldwide to teach dog training seminars, Denise writes prolifically for the dog sports audience, and she also runs a very successful online school for competition dog sports - the Fenzi Dog Sports Academy. You can find all of her books at www.thedogathlete.com, her school at www.fenzidogsportsacademy.com, and her blog at www.denisefenzipetdogs.com

Preface

Are you making choices for your dog based on both his stage of training and his unique temperament? Are you handling your dog in a manner that builds on his strengths while also improving his weaknesses? Or are you following someone else's training plan that may or may not have anything to do with what your dog needs?

If you want to understand how your dog's temperament is reflected in his behavior, and how that should impact your training decisions, this book is for you. In the pages that lie ahead, we will consider who your dog actually is, not who you think he "should" be. We will explore a range of traits your dog might have and how those traits impact the way your dog responds to training. We'll consider our options for working with these traits, both individually and in concert with other traits, in order to enhance our chances of developing an excellent working partner.

This isn't your typical dog training book with a cookie-cutter approach. Generic dog training is only a good idea if you happen to have a generic dog, and most dogs are not generic at all! It makes no sense to focus on drive building activities with a dog who is already frantic and out of his head with excitement over what you have to offer. It is equally illogical to work through self-control exercises with a dog who has never shown any indication that he even wants what you have to offer in exchange for his efforts.

My goal is to help you develop a dog who is as secure and receptive to training as possible; one who is engaged with you and with what you are doing together. To get there, you need to understand who your dog is. From that point of understanding, you can appropriately structure your training sessions to develop a willing and engaged partner.

In other words: Train the dog in front of you!

Please note that the title of this book is not "How to Create a Doggy Miracle." If you purchased this book because your dog isn't on board with your current training plan and that's annoying you, this book is not likely to help much. This book is about tailoring training to your individual dog, not changing your dog to fit your ideas about training. If you can redefine success as bringing out the best in whatever dog you happen to have, this book will be extremely valuable to you.

A Note about Structure
In this book, I have ARTIFICIALLY divided traits into tidy little packages. I have written about things like working drive, confidence levels, and what your dog prefers to focus on. Unfortunately, there are problems with this approach; temperament and related behaviors are NOT tidy little packages. While temperament is largely fixed, behavior is quite fluid and will change depending on the dog's life experiences and specific circumstances. That makes answering questions such as, "Is this dog high or low in working drive?" quite difficult, even though the underlying quality of drive is largely innate. The dog's behavior simply depends on too many factors, like where you're training, who else is present, and what you're using as a motivator. This list of modifiers goes on and on, all of which will influence the dog's expression of temperament at any given time. As a result, the constantly shifting interplay between life experience, temperament, and the specific circumstances can make the expressed behaviors

appear endlessly changeable.

So why bother at all? Well, with time and experience, you can learn to combine your dog's qualities in your mind and make predictions that will help you maximize your dog's wellbeing. For example, if you know that your handler-focused, sensitive, driven working dog fails to function well at the local park, then you know that the relevant variable is the environment, not your dog's love of work. In that case, there is no reason to focus on building working drive. Your time will be better spent focusing on developing your dog's confidence in public. Creating categories of temperament traits is extremely valuable if it helps you understand your dog better, and if you use that information to make better decisions for your dog. On the other hand, creating categories of temperament is a problem if it causes you to lock your dog into a box without paying attention to what is actually happening in front of you at a specific moment in time.

Dogs are not so different in this regard from people. For example, are you an introvert or an extrovert? On balance, you might have more traits that make you answer that question one way or the other, but when you consider the details, you probably find that the answer gets muddy. What is your behavior like in small groups? Large groups? And are your answers different if the groups are made up of familiar people rather than strangers? Your behavior, while still a reflection of your underlying temperament, can shift all the time based on the specific circumstances. And yet most of us still identify primarily as an introvert or an extrovert.

And so it goes with our dogs.

Train the dog in front of you and see what happens. Remain flexible and open-minded. If you do, you might just discover a depth of enjoyment and passion for your dog that you had no idea was possible!

Chapter One
Good Dogs and Bad Dogs

© Patrick Powers Photography

There are many dogs in the world; some are incredibly accomplished, while others happily ignore their owners. Despite this, there are no "good" dogs or "bad" dogs. There are just dogs, and each has his own unique strengths and weaknesses. For those of us interested in dog sports, we sometimes long wistfully for our dogs to magically transform into perfect, high energy, confident, and engaged working partners, while also remaining calm, easy, and loving in the house - even though we know that's not realistic. And if you are one of those incredibly rare folks that do have that dog, well… hold on tight and thank your lucky stars!

Instead of wishing for that magical dog, think about how you might create a dog who is receptive to training. What we want are those dogs who, through temperament or training, have just the right amount of the qualities that we need for training. For example, some dogs struggle with self-control, often because they want what you have. Other dogs may have no self-control issues at all; not because they have amazing self-control, but because they don't care about your motivators. Both of those types of dogs are challenging to train, but for very different reasons which have nothing to do with them being "good" or "bad."

To get that "just right" dog, the handler must learn what her dog needs and how to provide for that. Part of that will include specific training; higher drive dogs are worked to develop self-control and lower drive dogs are worked to build their love for the motivators. As a result, both types of dogs become more receptive to training.

While you cannot change a dog's basic temperament, you can emphasize training that benefits your specific team. Over time you might find that you do such a good job that people who see the end result think your dog was born that way, without recognizing the efforts you put in to get your dog there!

No Bad Dogs

For every strength that your dog brings, you can assume that there is a weakness that partners with it. And to further complicate this matter, you can also assume that your dog's traits are being influenced by other factors such as the environment, prior experiences, and training choices that you are making each and every day. To understand how this works, let's look at some of my dogs.

Cisu

Cisu was a mentally tough dog. Right from puppyhood, she was confident, curious, and powerful; she was unfazed by the chaos of the dog show world. When she did exhibit stress, she would stress up and become extremely handler focused, so she looked even flashier while working than she did when she was relaxed! On top of that, she was calm in the house and simply a joy to live with. In short, she appeared to be one of those rare "magical dogs."

Unfortunately, all of that confidence meant that she didn't need me very much at all. She was incredibly independent and self-determined. She was happy to hop out of a car and go for a walk, alone, and she wasn't likely to look back unless I called her to me. She was adept at calculating the value of what she wanted to do (explore, visit people, chase critters, etc.) against what I might have to offer as an alternative (food, toys, work, and my personality). If she decided it wasn't a fair trade, then I lost that round. Cisu wasn't concerned about "making me happy." She loved me and the things I offered just fine, but she loved lots of other options as well.

Cisu's independence and confidence were both her greatest challenge and her greatest strength. She may have seemed "magical," but it took a good deal of thought and work to get us where we could use those traits to our advantage as a working team. Ultimately, Cisu retired an AKC Obedience Trial Champion (OTCH), a Schutzhund 3 (SchH3) with all excellent scores, an advanced tracking dog with an excellent score (FH), and AKC Tracking Dog (TD).

Was Cisu a good dog or a bad dog?

Raika

Raika was born an energetic bundle of drive, energy, focus, and desire to please. She never took her eyes off me or strayed far from where I happened to be. She was hardworking, focused, and enthusiastic regardless of what I had to offer in exchange for her efforts. In many ways she was the polar opposite of Cisu.

Unfortunately, all of that focus and desire to please was rooted in a basic uncertainty about the world and her own inability to feel secure without a person to support her. Raika was an anxious dog who could not manage her behavior or emotions without constant support. She needed leadership to be a "whole" dog. Without a human present, she was nervous and stressed. This made her hard to show and hard to live with.

Competition was incredibly stressful for Raika, and at first she failed to function anywhere near the level that I believed she was trained for. We did eventually work through most of her issues, but it was time intensive and laborious. She may have been focused and dependent, but it came from an anxious temperament rather than from a place of strength and confidence. Ultimately, though, Raika retired as an AKC Obedience Trial Champion (OTCH), Schutzhund 2 (SchH2), Mondio Ring 1 (MR1), and AKC Tracking Dog (TD).

Was Raika a good dog or a bad dog?

Brito and Lyra

Brito is bold, inquisitive, and comfortable in a wide variety of new environments, generally marching right into a new space with his tail in the air. He has a good nature and basically calm temperament (until he's not!), and he cares about not displeasing me when he is engaged (which is not the same as caring about pleasing me). Brito enjoys the company of people and is rarely upset or disturbed by objects in the environment;

indeed, he loves to explore them directly. He enjoys food and toys equally, though his drives for those things are innately modest.

But despite all these great qualities, Brito struggles to ignore the call of the world when working. He is easily drawn to any changes in the environment, and he will impulsively take off to investigate novel stimuli. He cannot be trusted off leash in a variety of environments due to his impulsive nature. He can be reactive toward dogs and he is easily triggered to lose self-control in the presence of fast movement. He is slow to learn skills, will not persist under pressure, and has a poor ability to generalize. A retrieve in the house looks nothing like a retrieve in the yard - at least not to Brito.

Meanwhile, Lyra is extremely social and good-natured. She enjoys both people and dogs, and has naturally excellent interactive skills. She enjoys playing ball and tug, and with age she has developed a reasonable level of food drive. She loves going new places to explore. She is extremely quick to learn new skills and has no trouble generalizing those skills to new environments. Lyra is very cooperative and wants to get along.

Lyra's environmental focus is very strong; there are few things that she enjoys more than exploring a new space with both her nose and her eyes. When she is engaged with the environment her interest in classic motivators such as food or toys drops to almost zero; she will spit out almost anything that is offered to her until she has fully satiated on a training location. For Lyra, every location is a new location, even her own training yard!

Brito and Lyra have just begun their trial careers with the new TEAM obedience titles, so we have a long way to go before we'll know what we will or will not accomplish in competition before they reach retirement. What I can say is that both Brito and Lyra are good dogs, just like every dog I've ever trained. Yes, they bring challenges, but they also bring strengths. It's up to me to bring out the best in them.

Temperament and Behavior Packages

Using the four dogs above, can you see how there are no good dogs or bad dogs, just tendencies, packages, and tradeoffs? If Cisu were dependent on me, I could have created a team player much more quickly, but would she have shown so much confidence when working through exercises that required independent thought? If Raika had been less dependent on me, would she have worked so hard to please me and stay in my good graces, even when I had relatively little to offer in return? If Brito were less confident, I could probably trust him to stay close to me off leash - but would he be so secure in new environments?

As my dogs exemplify so well, dogs tend to show packages of temperament types and behavior, and most traits have both good and bad components for those of us training for dog sports. But it's still just temperament and behavior; it's not good or bad, it just is. By understanding the package of tendencies that each of my dogs bring to the training ring, I can quickly and easily set up appropriate training sessions.

This book is intended to help you form a clear mental model of your dog so you too can make the best of what your dog has to offer. For example, when you arrive at a park to train and see that a soccer game is in progress, a solid knowledge of who your dog is will either cause you to dismiss the soccer game as a concern and continue on with your training plan, pack up the car and head home, or, most likely, allow you to pick an appropriate middle ground that will help your dog become stronger and more confident over time.

Who is Your Dog TODAY?

Speaking of becoming "stronger and more confident over time"... When thinking about who our dogs are, it's incredibly important that we continually check our mental model against the dog standing in front of us. Dogs are constantly changing as a result of both our training and the effects of time, age, and maturity. Even though most of us know that on some level, it is still easy to get stuck in our outdated assessments. Are you training your dog as he is today, or are you training the puppy he used to be?

Keep this in mind both as you work through this book, and as you reflect on who your dog is a week, month, or even a year from now.

Chapter Two

Secure Dogs and Cautious Dogs

 The first set of traits we will consider is secure versus cautious. Keep in mind that this, like all of the traits we will consider in this book, tends to fall somewhere on a continuum. No dog is perfectly secure nor completely cautious. Still, he will tend to fall more on one side than the other.

Is Your Dog Secure or Cautious?

Secure dogs will normally eat, play, and explore at a distance from their handlers in new environments or in the presence of novel stimuli. These dogs will work and interact pretty much anywhere and anytime; all you have to do is pull out some high quality motivators and away you go!

While there may be times they choose not to interact with you, that choice is driven by the relative value of the alternatives, not because the dog is fearful of what's going on around him. If you take your secure dog to a new park to train, he might choose to chase the squirrels instead of interact with you because those squirrels are just so interesting! However, if you have his favorite snack - say, hot dogs, which he rates as a 9 out of 10 on the scale of awesome things - and his interest in squirrels is only an 8 - you will be able to do some training.

Cautious dogs, on the other hand, may range from mildly cautious to insecure and nervous to downright scared. Depending on where on the cautious spectrum your dog falls, when you take him to a new environment, he might startle at things but recover fairly quickly; he might start jumping on you, grabbing at your clothes frantically, or simply move around quickly and without purpose; he might become a wide-eyed wallflower, not moving much at all; or he might even become so overwhelmed that he lies down and appears catatonic.

In all of these cases, your training trip to the park will not go well. It doesn't matter how wonderful your treats are because fear always trumps motivation. Even if he's willing to take your cookies, your dog will not be fully engaged with you. Trying to teach specific skills will be pointless.

Two Different Training Approaches

The primary tendency your dog shows on the secure versus cautious continuum will determine your general approach to training.

For secure dogs, your training approach will be relatively straightforward. Your goal will be to teach your dog tiny snippets of behavior in public right from the start. You want your dog to learn early on how to work with focus and engagement, even in chaotic places. To do this, you'll need to learn how to balance the attractiveness of the environment with the attractiveness of what you have to offer: food, toys, and your winning personality!

For example, if the package of things you bring to the table creates a value of 8 out of 10, you need to ensure that the environment you choose to train in is lower than that. This will mean that you need to balance the intensity of what is going on around you with your proximity to it. Training next to the tennis courts during a high-energy match with a ball-obsessed dog will probably make the environment a 10 out of 10. How far away do you need to move to take that down to a 6 out of 10?

Continually evaluate the relative worth of the environment and what you have to offer. As time goes by, your dog may become less interested in what you are doing together, and your value as an 8 may drop! If your dog's enthusiasm for engaging with you falls below a 6 (the value of the environment), you will begin to struggle. Keep your training sessions short enough that this doesn't happen!

With a secure dog, it's fine to overwhelm environmental excitement with excellent food, toys, and personality from time to time, but with an insecure dog, that is a recipe for a very stressed and nervous competition dog down the road. This is why your overall training approach for a cautious dog will be quite different. Your goal will be to help your dog become more secure in new environments, not to train skills.

This is important because many worried dogs will work if you ask. For example, dogs whose concern about the environment is a 5 out of 10 will train with you if the package of food, toys, and personality you bring are an 8. However, doing so is a mistake. When a dog is nervous or worried and you train anyway, progress is painfully slow because the dog must emotionally multitask, and that is exhausting. Can you imagine trying to learn a new skill when you are thinking about your sick child at home (emotional distress), when you have a headache (physical pain), or when you think a bad person might be following you (fear)?

Acclimation is vitally important for cautious dogs. Acclimation is the process of helping your dog adapt to a new environment by allowing him to take in all the sights, sounds, and smells of the place. You can do this by allowing him to explore the area on leash until he feels more comfortable; this can take up to 20 minutes or even longer. (For more information on acclimation, please see the book I co-authored with Deb Jones, *Dog Sports Skills, Book 4: Focus and Engage!*)

However, even after acclimation, you should focus on play and engagement with your cautious dog instead of formal training skills. Training can happen at home; in public, you need to build up your dog's confidence and enthusiasm for working with you.

Can you see why it's critical to understand if your dog is generally secure or cautious before you start training in new places? Both types of dog might work for you in the moment, but only one type SHOULD be asked to work for you. The other dogs should be asked to explore and breathe and simply take it all in until they are truly ready to work without underlying worry or nervousness.

When Your Dog is More Extreme

Some dogs take things to an extreme. Some dogs are so hyper and excited by the world that thinking becomes impossible.

Others are so scared that they can't engage. In both cases, neither dog is ready to work.

Dogs who take being secure to the extreme aren't just confident, they're excited. In fact, they are so excited that they can't think. Can you imagine trying to learn a new skill when you are seeing the Grand Canyon for the first time? You would be so overwhelmed by what you're seeing that learning is simply impossible.

Acclimation often does wonders for these dogs as well, but you need to do it to the point of satiation, where the dog has worn off all of his excitement and is verging on boredom. This might mean waiting until he's been at the Grand Canyon for a week, or it might mean moving so far away that he can barely glimpse the Grand Canyon through the trees. Better yet, start somewhere far less interesting than the Grand Canyon entirely! Regardless of which approach you take, be sure that you provide interesting work, remain engaged in the process yourself, and create sufficient structure to keep your dog focused. If your dog never satiates or manages to focus under specific high-arousal circumstances, don't worry. We'll talk about more options in the chapter on obsessiveness.

On the other hand, some dogs take cautiousness to the opposite extreme. They exhibit fear in life as a whole, not just in new environments. They don't have a place they can rely on for strength and comfort. In fact, any change to the world throws them into a tailspin. Buy a new couch? Dog panics. Offer a new toy? Dog runs off. Children make noise outside? Dog hides in your closet.

Training these dogs is an excellent idea! Short sessions of free shaping with a very high rate of reinforcement can give them a good boost of confidence. Shaping, games, puzzle toys - anything to help these dogs build up confidence in their own homes. The question really isn't whether you should train these dogs; the question is whether you should compete with them.

If you can train without pressure and with no particular goals, your dog may become comfortable enough that you can compete with him - probably in a low stress and relaxed competition venue. However, if you have a competitive drive to teach skills and win big, the odds are quite good that the pressure you end up putting on your dog will not only prevent you from progressing towards your competition goals, but worse, that pressure will make it harder and harder for this dog to relax and enjoy life at all.

Not every dog can or should be prepared for competition, but all dogs can benefit from positive and respectful training where creating success is the primary focus. If your sincere efforts do not seem to be helping, or if they appear to be causing harm, then stop training and strongly consider a trip to a veterinary behaviorist to discuss all of your options.

It Depends...

Although your dog will likely be more secure or more cautious as a matter of temperament, it's important to point out that there are other factors at play. Your assessment might change depending on the environment your dog is in. Your dog may be secure in some environments, but cautious in others. He might be too excited to work in some places, but not in others. For example, if sounds bother your dog, but visual stimuli are no trouble at all, then your dog will be secure in the busy park but insecure near the open firing range. That's fine - handle each environment as it comes, changing your plan as appropriate. When you can do that, you are truly training the dog in front of you!

Chapter Three

Handler Focused Dogs and Environmental Dogs

The next set of traits to consider is whether a dog is typically more focused on his handler or on the environment. Handler focused means the dog is focused on his person, while environmentally focused dogs tend to be more interested in other people, dogs, places, and things. Splitting the category like this is somewhat unusual. In the previous chapter, we talked about dogs being secure or cautious, and the clear ideal was to have a more secure dog. However, when it comes to focus, I prefer that a dog is both handler focused and environmentally focused. This tends not to be intuitive to people; why in the world would I want an environmentally focused dog?

Dogs who have taken the time to focus on the environment are not likely to be taken by surprise. They've seen enough people, places, dogs, and things that they have generalized the idea that the world is a safe place. As a result, they often find it much easier to focus on their handler with 100% confidence and assurance when it is time to work.

At the same time, I want a dog who recognizes that the handler is the source of great stuff like food, toys, and interaction! After the initial puppy phase (which lasts up to approximately 2 years of age), I want the dog to show a clear choice for handler interaction and work. However, I only expect this after the dog has taken a reasonable amount of time in new environments to ensure his feelings of safety and to satisfy any basic curiosity.

Handler Focused or Environmentally Focused?

Not sure if your dog is more handler focused or environmentally focused? Here's a super quick test to tell.

Take your dog to a new (safe) place. Without saying anything, let your dog out of the car either without a leash or on a long line. (If your dog has been trained to re-orient to you after getting out of the car, you may need to give a release cue so he knows that he is free to choose at this time.) What happens? Does he turn back and wait for you, explore a nearby area with an eye on you, or zip off? How far does he go if you don't call him back?

Your answers will help you determine your dog's levels of handler focus and environmental focus - at least at this particular time and in this particular place. Remember, although the traits we're discussing in this book tend to be stable, many factors can impact the way they are expressed. Always be willing to revise your assessment of your dog.

Environmental Focus: Curiosity or Fear?

If your dog is more focused on the environment, it's critical to know WHY. Is he curious or is he nervous? It's actually quite easy to mistake fear for curiosity, so it's important to pay careful attention to your dog's overall demeanor, his body language, and how he responds to redirection.

Dogs who are focused on the environment because they are curious tend to be curious in life as a whole. Confident dogs may move around a lot, but they move with purpose and sureness. If you redirect your dog and he stays focused on you with his ears up and looks at you without taking any quick glances around, then he's probably just curious about the world.

Meanwhile, dogs with fear issues will often show a basic nervousness in life. Nervous or worried dogs tend to check in and out, causing them to struggle with accuracy in work when in new places. Their ears usually flick around, their tails are held low, and when they look around, they tend to stare at one thing for long periods of time or constantly scan the environment. Their energy levels are either unusually high or abnormally low. They might pant or leave wet footprints, even when it's cool out. Redirecting fearful or nervous dogs with food or toys is generally a mistake, as discussed in chapter two.

Complicating matters, there are plenty of dogs who are both - they are very curious about what is out there, but they are nervous about it at the same time! Dogs who are both curious and nervous are challenging because they are easily overwhelmed, but have no desire to leave. They want to see what's going on, yet they do not handle the novelty well.

In general, if your dog is fearful, you'll need to figure out what categories of things upset your dog, and then expose him to those things in tiny doses and from a sufficient distance that your dog appears comfortable and even downright bored. It doesn't matter WHAT bothers your dog - people, places, dogs, or things - the process is the same. If you're struggling to figure out how to do this, work with a qualified behaviorist.

With curious dogs, you'll want to do most of your initial training in a simple and quiet environment where your dog can focus easily. However, depending on what is striking your dog's curiosity, your approach might change just a bit. Let's look at the most common causes of curiosity in environmentally focused dogs, and what you can do about it.

Curious about People

Dogs who are environmentally focused because they are curious are often hyper social. If you're fortunate enough to recognize this tendency in your puppy, you can save yourself a lot of grief by teaching your puppy that only calm behavior gets him attention. Very social puppies do NOT need a lot of squealing and squeaking people fussing over them. Instead, they need to learn early on that people ignore them until they are calm. Remember, socialization means exposure, not interaction.

If you already have an adult dog who is hyper social, he's probably developed a range of issues greeting people as a result. These dogs tend to go hard and fast at people. They almost always look right up into the approaching person's face and then lunge forwards, sometimes mouthing or climbing their way up the person.

Needless to say, this type of dog is rarely appreciated by the victim. In addition, curbing this behavior is very difficult, and even a calm owner is going to have a really hard time hiding her frustration with this behavior. Holding the dog down simply builds his drive to launch into the person's face. Dropping food often does not work because these dogs are fast; they eat and then launch, or they leave most of the food behind and go for the person instead. Turning your back has no effect at all; the dog simply claws your back or grabs your hair. What usually ends up happening is that the dog is strongly disciplined, which creates conflict for the dog. Rather than subduing him, the punishment causes the problem behavior to become even more frantic.

With these dogs, just the mere sight of a person will send them over threshold; they are unable to make good, rational decisions about their behavior. Unfortunately, training requires a rational participant who can figure out how to adjust his behavior in order to maximize good things and minimize bad things, which means that training is often futile. Worse, the more time a dog spends over threshold, the more easily he will end up in this bad place, creating a nasty cycle. This happens because the hyper greeter isn't a happy dog who loves everyone. The hyper greeter is a dog who has an uncontrollable need to visit people, even when he realizes that people do not like his behavior. This leads to conflict, and conflict causes the dog to go over threshold.

There is hope for these dogs, but it is going to take significant work on your part. While working on this behavior, you MUST manage the dog. This is nonnegotiable, as every episode of failure will exacerbate your dog's behavior and increase your own frustration. Keep your dog on a front clip harness when people are around and do NOT allow your dog to get to them. Crate your dog when people come to your house.

Now, enlist a dog savvy helper. Your helper's job will be to use a high value cookie to distract the dog from interacting with him. The helper should NOT give the cookie to the dog at any point; it is for distraction only! This is why the helper must be a dog savvy person; the temptation to give the dog the cookie will be too much for anyone else.

Allow the dog to approach the helper, either loose or on a leash. As soon as the dog reaches the helper, the helper will "magnetize" the dog by holding the cookie at the level of the dog's head. The cookie should redirect the dog's focus and energy from the helper's face to the food. Any time the dog looks at the helper's face, the helper should use her free hand as a visual barrier. This whole process will be easier if the helper is neutral, casual, and quiet.

Some dogs, when they realize that the helper isn't giving them the cookie, will go back to leaping at the person's face. If that happens, make the cookie a bit more "active" to keep the dog focused on it. It's important that the helper work hard to keep the dog's attention on the cookie and off her face or this method will not work. If the dog is mouthy, the handler should make a fist with the cookie inside and keep the back of her hand facing the dog.

There isn't much for you to do except wait. If you chose to have your dog on leash, you must ensure there is no tension on the leash. We want the dog operating on his own power and showing self-control without external constraints.

At some point, your dog will likely turn back to you. The instant this happens, give your dog a cookie of equal value and praise him like crazy. Then encourage your dog to return to your helper, where the process is repeated. When the dog is barely willing to engage the helper anymore because he's realized the helper isn't much fun, you can allow the helper to quietly interact with your dog, but only if you're in a non-competition setting. If the dog becomes excited, the helper should use the cookie to redirect the dog away from interaction.

If your dog does not show any interest in turning back to you, you can make some small sounds or use another cookie to lure the dog back to you and then repeat. Although it's preferable for the dog to choose to turn back to you on his own, by using this technique, most dogs will quickly learn to turn back to you especially if they have previously been taught a re-orienting behavior.

Soon, you will find that your helper no longer requires a cookie – simply holding out her hands as if she had one is enough to cue the dog to turn back to you. And since success allows the dog to stay calm and under threshold, the dog will soon learn that he can be near people without losing control – an excellent end result!

I have had extremely good success with this method, but as with all behavior work, it requires consistency in the application and management the rest of the time. However, this method is NOT appropriate for fearful dogs who bounce off the new person, backing up and barking hysterically, or dogs who alternate between extreme greeting behaviors and nervous nipping or barking at a new person. Fearful dogs should not be allowed to approach new people until they show the ability to do so in a positive frame of mind.

Curious about Dogs

It is incredibly difficult to work with dogs who are attracted to other dogs because the other dogs have rights too! Just because your dog wants to meet and greet doesn't mean the other dog will - or that his person will want him to visit. Plus, it's much harder to get a helper dog to cooperate like you did for dogs who really want to visit people.

Your goal will be the same as if your dog was afraid of other dogs: to teach him to be calm and relaxed in the presence of other dogs. In both cases, you'll need to work under threshold by being so far away that your dog can remain calm while he works or plays with you.

Another really helpful tool is to teach your dog to "go to mat." This behavior gives your dog a specific thing to do in the face of attractive alternatives. Instead of asking yourself what you don't want your dog to do ("I don't want my dog lunging towards that other dog!"), ask yourself what you do want. Really, any behavior that's incompatible with lunging towards another dog will work, but "go to mat" is concrete and clear, allows the dog to look at the other dog without reacting, and has the added bonus of being incredibly portable.

Teaching a mat behavior is easy; simply reward your dog for staying on his mat with a steady stream of treats until released. It's easiest to do this at home when nothing else is going on because there are no other interesting alternatives competing for his interest. Gradually lengthen the time between treats. Once he's doing well with that, start adding challenges (and increasing the number of cookies you give him when you do!). Can your dog stay on the mat when the doorbell rings? When you leave the room briefly? When a bowl of food is sitting on the table nearby? How about that bowl of food on the floor? The stronger your dog's commitment to that mat at home, the more useful it will be when you take it out into public.

When you do take this behavior out into public for the first time, be sure to start far away from the other dog. As your dog shows the ability to relax on his mat even when new dogs are far away, start moving his mat closer to the trigger dogs.

This process can be time consuming but your choices are quite limited. If you try to force your dog to accept other dogs and remain calm (through punishment), you may create the illusion of calmness, but he's likely just shutting down instead. This doesn't solve the underlying issue, and worse, it often creates conflict or even fear in your dog, both of which will negatively affect any training that you attempt at that time.

<u>Curious about the Environment</u>

Finally, for those dogs who are simply curious about everything in the environment, you have two basic options: acclimation and satiation.

As we already discussed in the previous chapter, acclimation means "to settle in." In this process, the dog becomes familiar and comfortable with the environment. Allowing for acclimation is just good training; grabbing a dog from a crate and expecting focused work and attention when the dog has not had a chance to orient to the environment is unreasonable. The hard part is getting the humans to do it! Humans tend to be in a hurry, and that extra ten minutes is not part of the schedule. For dogs who are only mildly nervous or curious but also very motivated by either work or classic motivators, acclimation is plenty. Likewise, dogs who have lower energy levels also do just fine with acclimation alone. Simply walk the dog through the working space, then wait for the dog to engage.

Satiation is an extension of acclimation, and includes completely exhausting the dog's interest in the environment. Satiation does not make sense for all dogs, but some will benefit greatly from it. This include dogs with significant nervousness or curiosity, dogs who aren't very interested in work or classic motivators, and dogs who have enough stamina to participate in satiation and then work afterwards. You'll know that your dog will benefit from satiation if he tends to check in and out of work, or if he focuses when close to you and your reinforcers but either drifts, sniffs, or multitasks at a distance.

Satiation is time-intensive. You are not going to stand around and wait for your dog to check in with you. Instead, you'll allow your dog to explore - for a very long time. This can be done either on leash or off, depending on safety and size of the area. And you'll do this until your dog is truly done. The stronger your dog's interest in the world, the longer this will take. It's not even a matter of minutes or hours – it can be days. You may need to return to the same place over and over and not do much of anything for thirty minutes or so.

You'll know your dog has satiated if he lies down to take a nap, or becomes quite insistent that he'd like to do something else. That is where you can step in. NOW is the time to ask your dog to work, and make it worthwhile! Keep the work interesting and be fully engaged yourself! Do not allow your dog to check in and out - if you need to call him back more than once or twice, it's time to end the training session.

Sometimes, dogs with high levels of environmental curiosity respond differently. Instead of getting bored, they seem to become even MORE absorbed in the world and even LESS interested in work. For these dogs, you'll need to use an enforced long down for the purposes of acclimation without interaction.

Start by walking for a few minutes for basic acclimation, then put your dog on a long down. The dog is no longer allowed to actively explore, but he is still given as much time as needed to take everything in. Don't worry, you won't be there forever; it is a rare dog who can entertain himself for more than twenty minutes while lying in one spot. You may give the dog low value treats during the long down, but try to reserve the really good treats for the working period that is to follow.

After the very long down, how is your dog's work? If the work is better, then you're on the right track! Over time, that long down should be for shorter and shorter periods of time as your dog learns the routine. But if your dog loses focus while working, or if you feel like he just needs a break, go ahead and do another long down! It's not a punishment; it's a chance for him to clear his head and refocus on his work with you.

Environmentally Focused... or Handler Avoidance?

Some dogs who appear environmentally focused are actually practicing handler avoidance. While this is an unattractive reality, some handlers put so much pressure on their dogs to work and to stay focused on them (either intentionally or inadvertently) that the dogs become desperate to escape. They turn to the environment, not because they are attracted to it, but because they associate the handler with so much pressure. It doesn't matter if the owner thinks she's being "fun." What matters is the dog's opinion.

If you've created a situation where your dog watches you because you have trained him to do so ("playfully" pulling his hair if he looks away, getting louder and more exciting, waving a toy in front of his face, or crating the dog to "teach" him not to avoid training), then you probably have a dog who appears handler focused but has actually disengaged mentally.

If you're not sure if this is your dog, try this: Work your dog for a short while and then release him to choose what he wants to do next. If your dog leaves and does not come back until you specifically instruct him to do so, it is possible that your dog does not want to work with you at all. He might appear focused because he has learned that failure to engage leads to unpleasant consequences, but it's more of a "lights on but no one's home" phenomenon.

The solution is not difficult. Allow your dog to breathe. Work on matching your energy in training to your dog's energy; if your dog is showing an energy level of 5, do not come in whooping and hollering with a 10 in a desperate effort to make your dog interested in you. Instead, work on engagement training to the point that your dog recognizes that work is a choice. The book *Dog Sports Skills, Book 4: Focus and Engage!* will be of great value.

Handler Focused

Now let's consider dogs who show a lot of handler focus when we do our simple "hop out of the car and see what happens" test. These dogs often prefer to stare at the handler and push for interaction. They might sniff around a bit, but it wouldn't occur to them to take a walk without you.

On the surface, this seems great. Dogs who are handler focused because they are enthusiastic to hang out or work with you are a joy to train. But sometimes, being handler focused is less about enthusiasm and more about being worried and lacking confidence. In these cases, the dog's focus on you is actually because he's asking you for help. You'll know if this is the case for your dog if he punctuates his staring at you with jumping at you with a frantic edge, or taking frequent and quick glances around.

If your dog is handler focused because of nervousness, you need to provide support to your dog! Pet him, allow him to sit close to you, move further away from the upsetting triggers, or change the environment altogether. But whatever you do, do NOT train a dog who is nervous. Take care of his discomfort first. The alternative is that your dog may learn to work in a stressed state. While that does work (especially with dogs who also have a high level of working drive), it's risky; in most competition rings you can't use food, toys, or constant interaction to help your dog feel better. These dogs often cave under the pressure of higher level competition or when problem solving is required at a distance from the handler. Instead of training your nervous, high-drive dog, teach him that he is strong on his own four feet!

Some dogs are handler focused because they have been trained to stare at their trainers when in stressful or overwhelming conditions. If this is your dog, I'm going to suggest something radical: undo that training. I want you to actively encourage your dog to break contact with you and to start looking at the world. This may seem counterintuitive, but when you think about how acclimation works, it makes perfect sense.

In acclimation, your dog looks at the world until he is satisfied that the world is a safe place. He can't do that if you keep distracting him with food, toys, or work! If he never gets to look around and realize that he is perfectly safe, then he is reliant on you and your motivators for emotional support. While dogs can learn to work with a constant low (or high) level of anxiety, this anxiety becomes associated with work because of classical conditioning. This is not healthy. While redirecting your dog away from fear is a fine short-term management strategy to keep you out of trouble, long term you want your dog to be comfortable in the world and working because work is fun, not because it keeps the scary ghosts away.

If your nervous dog is so high drive that he won't look around or leave you, use an enforced long down at the start of each training session. When your dog understands that "waiting" is the first step before work, he's likely to start looking around - and feeling safer as a result!

By the way, even if your handler focused dog is handler focused because he likes to work, acclimation is still a fine idea. He doesn't need to interact with the world by visiting or sniffing every nook and cranny; a solid visual inspection will do. If necessary, an enforced long down may help.

So Who is Your Dog?

Whether your dog is environmental (out of either fear or curiosity), or handler focused (out of either fear or desire to work), or balanced (curious but easily redirected to handler focus through training opportunities), or in active handler avoidance (either watching the handler to avoid discipline, or taking every opportunity to get away when it's possible), remember that it can change! Be ready to reassess what your dog is telling you and to make a new plan based on what you know.

Chapter Four

Obsessive Dogs and Flexible Dogs

Imagine this: You are taking your dog for a walk when he finds a half eaten hamburger on the ground! Unfortunately for your dog, you see it a fraction of a second before he does, and you are able to prevent him from getting to it. He looks at it mournfully for another few seconds and then...

What happens next?

Does your dog give it one last glance and then continue on with you, ready for the next adventure? If so, your dog is flexible. He's easy going and willing to find entertainment in a variety of directions and odds are that he's also pretty biddable and willing to cooperate with you.

If, on the other hand, your dog's reaction is to dig in for all he's worth, desperately pedaling in place to get to the hamburger, then you either have a training issue, or you have a dog with a very persistent - and perhaps even obsessive - personality.

Obsessive dogs are the ones who keeping trying to turn around and go back to the hamburger. They are the ones who, weeks later, remember where that hamburger was and start pulling towards it when you're blocks away. They are the dogs whose brains get stuck long after you've forgotten the hamburger even existed.

Obsessive dogs can obsess about everything or only specific things. Food is a common one, of course, but maybe your dog obsesses over people or other dogs. If you do not allow your dog to greet someone, is he still looking wistfully in that direction twenty minutes later? Maybe your dog obsesses over toys. When you put a toy away during training, does your dog's brain seem to go away, too? Or maybe your dog obsesses about sex... or critters... or smelling things... or maybe he obsesses about all of these things, and more!

If you're not sure if your dog is obsessive, put your dog on a very long down stay near something attractive. Go ahead and reward your dog frequently for that down stay, but notice how your dog's behavior changes. If he got bored relatively quickly, started looking to you for a cookie or something to do, then your dog is fairly flexible. General acclimation, satiation, or a long down are the tools you'll need to help your dog adjust to new situations. But if your dog starts to whine, stare, and get more worked up, well, this chapter is for you!

Handler Control

One approach to dealing with obsessive dogs is for the handler to be extremely controlling and keep the dog structured at all times. The dog is either performing a specific behavior, is on a long stay, or is in a crate. There is NO downtime during work, and the handler is paying attention every second, watching to catch the first second of any loss of attention and redirecting the dog back to work.

This approach can work, especially with a more biddable and stable dog who wants your motivators, but it's exhausting for the trainer. It's also a form of pressure-based training because the handler instantly calls the dog's name to bring him back to work and the dog soon learns that constant work is expected. Talk about pressure!

The goal with handler control is to prevent the obsessive behavior from starting and to offer an alternative that is relatively intense and fast paced. If this option is done well, the handler will still work the dog a good distance from whatever it is that the dog wants, make work as positive for the dog as possible, and will pay attention at every moment that the dog is working. This minimizes the pressure on the dog. In order to keep the work positive for the dog, the handler needs to know how much to ask for and for how long. In addition, the handler has to know when to take the dog out of the area entirely, and when to let the dog engage in what he wants to do for short periods of time before restarting the work.

Here's an example of what handler control might look like: The dog is allowed into the area where the distractions exist; let's say the distractions are squirrels in the trees. The dog is allowed basic acclimation time on leash, but only long enough to feel emotionally safe (no effort is being made to satiate here). After a few minutes, the handler moves a reasonable distance away, says the dog's name, and then works to keep her energy a notch above the dog's energy. The dog is moved quickly between working exercises, so the handler must plan in advance what they want to do. Any breaks involve either a down stay or crating the dog. Further, when the dog is released from that break, the team goes immediately into work again.

When using handler control, the pace and intensity of work tends to be on the high side. Further, each bout of work is likely to be short - only a few minutes - because then everyone needs a break, including the handler.

This approach works best when trial settings tend to be devoid of the specific distraction (indoor trials do not have squirrels in the trees) AND where the dog has a good amount of interest in the motivators the handler might have. This last part is key because the motivators, combined with the handler's personality, have to be able to overwhelm anything else that might be out there.

In my mind, this is not a very desirable option. Not only is this an exhausting approach for the handler, but the likelihood of it holding up in trial is usually poor. It's also easy to pressure the dog much too hard, which will cause the dog to dislike training altogether. There are better ways to work with obsessive dogs.

Premack

The Premack Principle is a fancy way of saying make a deal with your dog. If you do what I want, then I will give you what you want. For this to work, you need three things.

1. A dog who has enough brainpower left in the presence of the distraction that he can function at least a little bit, and -
2. A cue that is so extremely simple that your dog can actually do it, even when he's in the midst of an obsessive haze, and

3. A way to prevent unauthorized access to whatever the dog wants, whether this is a leash (control the dog!), a fence (control the thing!), or simply a cooperative dog.

From there, the idea is simple, in theory. Ask for the very easy behavior you identified in step two, and when your dog complies, let him have what he wants. The object of obsession becomes the reward for cooperation!

Of course, one of the challenges with obsessive dogs is that they struggle to function at all. Even performing the simplest behavior in the face of the object of obsession is such a challenge that it's hard for them to have enough success to recognize that cooperation is what does the trick. Using Premack with obsessive dogs often requires you to back up even further. Instead of asking for a sit, try asking them to put slack in the leash in order to get their reward. Or maybe instead of eye contact, they simply flick an ear in your direction. Regardless, you'll have to move very slowly with the more obsessive dogs. In fact, for this to work to the point where you can actually compete, you'll have to work so slowly and so carefully that there is no doubt in your dog's mind that cooperating with you is the only route to whatever he wants.

All dogs (flexible or otherwise) can be trained with Premack, but I use environmental rewards for competition behaviors as a last resort for a number of reasons. As already mentioned, it's time consuming. In addition, if it's not done in small enough increments, it often creates a lot of frustration in our dogs, which thwarts the very learning we were trying to accomplish. It's also inconvenient, if not downright impractical during competition (you can't allow your movement obsessed dog to go chasing after a fellow agility competitor!).

In my opinion, Premack is best used casually; I find that it works best with very simple behaviors, like making eye contact before opening a gate, as opposed to performing entire behavior chains in exchange for a chance to chase a squirrel. But it can work. And if your dog is of an obsessive temperament, you might find that it is the only option that truly causes your dog to choose to engage his brain and focus on what you want.

Let's Talk About Sex, Baby!

Dogs, like people, want sex. This is especially pronounced for intact dogs. Dogs can learn to work despite their hormones, and the approach you take will depend on your dog's general temperament.

Flexible Dogs

Flexible dogs are usually highly interested in either the work or the rewards that we are offering. As a result, they tend to be more biddable dogs who like to cooperate with their handlers. Generally, simply giving your dog a "not now" cue and offering an alternate activity will work. Highly flexible dogs will be fine with this; they tend to quickly forget about that female pee spot if you have interesting alternatives available.

Flexible dogs who aren't quite that easy going will benefit from this approach combined with acclimation and satiation; if they are frequently in the presence of females in various states of breeding readiness, they do, over time, come to terms with it. If you have a dog who is generally flexible, make a point of going to training environments and dog shows where you know there is a good chance of encountering intact females in various points of their reproductive cycle. After allowing the male to explore the smells to the point of satiation, and possibly to sniff (appropriately) girl dogs who are not in season, you may find that simple maturity and exposure is all it takes.

Even infrequent access to intact females will suffice. Allowing flexible dogs to satiate on the smells that are attracting them can work really well. They satisfy their curiosity, recognize that it's just pee (and not the girl herself), and that it's just not going to happen. So they give up, move on, and see what you have to offer.

Obsessive Dogs

Sometimes, exposure is not going to work. Some dogs will never satiate; access to what they wanted (in this example, sniffing where girls have been) BUILDS their drive and makes it harder and harder over time to redirect them back to what you want. They are unrelenting! This tends to be particularly true when the activity itself taps into a fundamental drive, like sex.

Here are your options:

Acclimation/Satiation

Because it's the easiest, try satiation first. Let your dog sniff, smell, and lick where the girls have been for as long as he wants. Recognize that he'll have to work his way through his teenage years before you can expect to see any real progress, so repeatedly doing satiation until he's two or three years old may be required.

Increase the Distance

A lot! Increase the distance between what your dog wants and where you choose to work. Girl dog in season? You'll be working down the block. Girl dog pee? You'll be working as far from the potty area as possible. Work on calm behaviors like lying on a mat - that may be the most complicated behavior your dog can perform for quite awhile!

Double Check Your Choice of Work and Motivators

Short work periods, high reward schedules, and quit before you use up every good brain cell in your dog's head! The more value you can build for the work itself, the better chance you'll have of getting your dog to focus on you. This isn't the time for complex chains that he hasn't mastered. Instead, focus on preferred activities with the best motivators you can find!

Handler Control

As we discussed earlier, working with your best motivators and using fast-paced work, push through as fast as you can, keeping the dog busy to the best of your ability. For the right dog, this can work, but it's hard on all parties involved and it is likely to fall apart in trial if the temptation is too close, where no motivators exist to distract him.

Premack

Make a deal with your dog. If you get some work then you'll let him check out the girl smells for a nice long time. If he wants to do even more smelling, then he needs to do more work.

Neutering

Neutered males tend to be much less obsessive about females, which makes sense. If sex drive is the root of your dog's obsessive behavior, then removing his hormones will allow him to relax and think about other motivators.

If the idea of taking away your dog's sex drive distresses you because it seems cruel to remove that pleasure, yet you never plan to breed him, then imagine being in a room with a full buffet while you are extremely hungry, but NEVER being allowed to eat any. Not even one bite. Would you prefer to have your food drive intact so that you can experience endless frustration and hunger, or simply have no food drive at all and take the issue off the table? In a nutshell, that's your intact, non-breeding, obsessive dog's life.

Corrections

It has to be discussed: Why not just correct your dog? The argument against corrections in this case is simple. Although you can fight over what the body is doing, you can't control the brain. Yes, your dog is staring right at you. But he's also thinking about the pee spot next to him. No, he doesn't respond to your hand signals because he's not really processing your cues. There's girl pee right there!

If you're doing simple, rote-style work which your dog can do with a split brain, or if you're working with a dog who is more flexible, driven, and biddable, then you might win. But as soon as the work requires real concentration, or if the dog is of a more obsessive temperament and has less working drive, then you will lose.

Besides, it's not much fun to train with corrections.

Is There Anything Good About Obsessive Dogs?

Yes! Obsessive dogs are unbeatable if you're interested in a working sport that uses a dog's natural drives. These dogs will stick it out when the weather is miserable, the day is long, and the training is poor. A flexible dog is much less likely to INSIST on working when conditions are not quite as appealing overall. So don't write off obsessive dogs; just work to end up on the same team!

Chapter Five

High Drive Dogs and Low Drive Dogs

In this chapter, we will analyze that often misunderstood term "working drive." Put simply, this is the dog's desire, willingness, and ability to work under a range of circumstances. The more a dog loves to work, pushes you to work, and accepts adversity within work (whether that is being wrong, coping with bad weather, resisting distractions, accepting reduced reinforcement, or so on), the more working drive we say a dog has.

Working drive is so tightly intertwined with the issue of motivation that it's extremely difficult to tease them apart. At their root, truly high drive dogs love to learn, work, and use their bodies - regardless of the motivator. However, since most training is accomplished with the strategic use of motivators, it can be very difficult to tell a dog who simply loves to work from a dog who is working strictly for the reward. Typically, it's only once you've been to several trials and your dog learns that no motivators will show up in competition that you can begin to tell the difference.

In this chapter, we will explore the characteristics of dogs who are both high and low in working drive. We'll discuss how you can identify which dog is which before you go to a show, and why they might be that way. Then we'll move on to discussing training techniques that will bring out the best in your dog, regardless of his level of working drive.

The Low Drive Dog

The term "low drive" covers a lot of territory, and the meaning varies wildly from one person to the other. Dogs with less working drive aren't terribly motivated by either classic motivators or the work itself. They are more easily distracted, less committed to work, and rarely show frustration behaviors because they never cared that much in the first place. Instead, when they are stressed or unsure of what they should do, they simply leave training, physically or mentally.

Why a Dog May Appear Low Drive

Although we often think of low drive as being a function of the dog's temperament, there is an enormous problem with this definition. Unlike physical traits like coat length or type, we cannot see drive - only the resulting behavior. We can observe that the dog is not behaving in a manner that we equate with a dog high in working drive, and so might conclude that this observable behavior is due to a temperament trait. But is it?

Worried Dogs

If you look back to the sections on worried, fearful, or anxious dogs, you'll see descriptions that are identical to the low drive dog. This is because dogs who are nervous often look low drive when they are really just shut down. If you help them feel better, you may find that this solves their so-called lack of drive.

A drive issue will be expressed regardless of the environment. If you've noticed that your dog is driven when training in familiar environments, but is not driven when he's in the world as a whole, then you do not have a drive problem. You do have a problem, but it is almost certainly related to the environment and not the dog's true drive for work.

Bored Dogs

Some dogs are trained in a long and drawn out manner with an emphasis on drills and routines. Both the handler and the dog seem to be going through the motions rather than interacting. These dogs might be slow to respond or uninterested in the task, but it's not because they are low drive. They're bored! This is especially likely if your dog tends to be high drive in one sport but low drive in another.

The key here is to realize you're in a rut and then restructure your training. Work new skills. Think up games. Change your motivators. Shorten your sessions. If your dog has a high drive/ low drive split between two or more sports, try to make your training time for the less desirable sport look more like the way you train for the favored sport. If your dog loves agility but hates obedience, maybe your dog wants to use his body! Emphasize lots of movement, speed, and quick changes of direction.

Low Power Dogs

Have you concluded that your dog is low drive because you get robotic responses rather than enthusiasm and speed? It might be that there's an imbalance in power between you and your dog. This often happens when a trainer uses a lot of corrections - even if that correction is simply an exasperated tone or an unhappy expression! Your dog may perceive that he has limited power to please you and so he has chosen to give up.

If your dog is extremely obedient, even when he doesn't want to cooperate; if people tell you that you're too hard on your dog; or if your dog prefers to work at a distance, leaving plenty of space between the two of you; your dog might be reacting to his lack of power. Skip ahead to the chapter on handler/dog power for a detailed analysis of your options.

Poor Training

Does your dog seem to love motivators like food and toys, but then shuts down as soon as they are introduced to training? Are you a relatively novice trainer? If you're struggling to apply good training, your dog is probably struggling to figure out what you want. This isn't a drive problem; it's simply a dog who is more sensitive to getting it right and who needs really good training! While the topic of training excellence is outside the scope of this book, knowing that this is the root issue should motivate you to improve and seek out resources to help you!

Using the Wrong Motivators

You cannot train with motivators that your dog doesn't want! While I am a huge fan of developing as many different motivators in training as possible, the fact is that you cannot use an option as a motivator unless your dog wants it. Make sure you build the dog's love of the motivator you've selected before you use it in training - or skip using it entirely.

This problem is especially common among trainers or philosophies that emphasize one form of motivation as being superior to other forms. Taken to an extreme, your motivator may actually become a punisher. Again, this is not a drive problem.

Curious Dogs

Being fascinated by the world does not mean your dog lacks drive to work and train, but it does mean that the value of the environment may be greater than what you have to offer. This creates obvious (and enormous!) challenges both for generalizing your training to new locations and for competing if it cannot be resolved.

Remember, a truly low drive dog will be low drive across the board - at all times and in all places. If your dog loves to work in quiet or familiar places but not in others, then you should be focused on reducing your dog's environmental interests through acclimation or satiation, not raising your dog's drive.

Health

Has your dog always shown a lack of interest in training or has there been a sudden or even gradual change? Are you noticing life changes as well? Any time you notice a change in your dog's behavior, consider that there might be an underlying health issue.

Unfortunately, our dogs cannot tell us when they don't feel well, and they are masters at disguising pain and sickness. Just because your dog is still able to run and participate in activities that he enjoys does not mean that he's not experiencing pain. Heck, who among us hasn't pretended that we were just fine when it suited us for a given situation? How many children INSIST that they can go to their friend's birthday party, even when they are so sick they can barely get out of bed?

The challenge with pain and sickness is that a trip to the veterinarian may or may not illuminate the issue. It is common for a dog with a serious issue like cancer or a brain tumor to come back with absolutely normal results on all tests - until the problem is so severe that very advanced tests are performed or the illness shows an obvious external manifestation.

Give your dog the benefit of the doubt. If he doesn't want to work, then let it go. There will always be another day.

Strategies for Working with Low Drive Dogs

If you've ruled out the issues above that cause dogs to appear low drive, even when they truly aren't, then you can try these strategies to encourage your dog to bring more energy and enthusiasm to your work together.

<u>Matching Your Dog's Energy</u>

When working with low drive dogs, people tend to start by putting out huge amounts of energy in order to "make" them want to play our games. Unfortunately, that is a recipe for failure. Coming in whooping and hollering is not likely to get you the response you're hoping for. Instead, you might scare your dog. You might drive your dog into classic avoidance. Or you might even force your dog to try to keep up with your energy because he's afraid of what you might do if he tries to leave. It is a rare situation when hitting your dog with toys or grabbing his fur to engage him is likely to get you a truly enthusiastic and willingly engaged partner.

If this describes your current approach, stop. Look at your dog's behavior. If your dog is showing you an energy level of 2 out of 10, go for a 3. This will look different for every dog; maybe you clap and smile, or maybe you even run out of the room in the hopes that he will chase you. But DO NOT go over the top wild and crazy. If you need help with this, please see the book I wrote with Deb Jones called *Dog Sports Skills, Book 3: Play!*

Structure Your Training Sessions for Success

Dogs with lower working drive should be trained less often and for shorter sessions. Compete less often as well. Use a higher reward schedule. Don't just hand over a cookie; make it an event! The emphasis in training should always be maximizing your dog's energy, enthusiasm, and movement. Use active rewards as much as possible; try throwing food and using play and toys to help your dog develop a love of active exercises. Ditch impulse control exercises altogether since low drive dogs are rarely impulsive. Your challenge is not going to be getting the dog to stop - your challenge will be getting your dog to go! Put 98% of your energy into "go"; tack on the "stop" later.

The Importance of Choice

We want your dog to opt in! Not because he'll starve to death or live in a crate if he chooses otherwise, but because you really do have interesting games to offer! Use the best motivators you can find to make it as likely as possible that your dog will choose to play your games. Focus on food and toys as "dessert" rather than "dinner." Ask for relatively little in return for a good payout. Focus on controlling the environment and the alternatives when you are working. Work for short periods! It's better to end training early than to have your dog develop a habit of walking away.

High Desire for Motivators but Low Interest In Work

Let's take a minute to consider dogs who show a high level of interest in motivators but a low interest in working for them, even with a very skilled trainer. These dogs really do want what you have, but they do not enjoy having to earn them. This is definitely unusual because most dogs (and people) enjoy using their brains to solve problems. Indeed, it is what separates dogs and people from many other species. These unique dogs get excited when they see that you have something for them! They WANT that cookie or toy! And then when you ask for something - even something simple like "sit" - they deflate completely. They appear to resent having to earn that cookie. They just want it. If they are hungry or really want it on that occasion, then they will work for it, but it's clearly a business transaction.

In situations like this, most determined trainers go for deprivation training. The dog learns that if he wants to eat, then he's going to have to earn it. This works! It also does nothing to build your relationship with your dog. You become a gatekeeper, not a partner.

Think of it like this. Let's say that your teenager wants money to buy fancy new designer shoes, so you suggest washing the car to earn some money. Most teenagers will respond in one of two ways. Either your teen will be happy to wash the car in order to get the money needed to buy his fancy shoes, or he'll just sit on the couch and feel resentful because he has to earn the money needed for the shoes; he'd rather have nothing than work for it. Now let's change the scenario a bit. What if these were not fancy designer shoes, but rather, the teen's shoes had worn out, the family had no money, and it was freezing outside. Now if the teen was offered a chance to earn those shoes, he'll probably do it. When absolute need is involved, and the relationships are clear (earn money and have shoes or don't earn money and have cold feet) then pretty much all of us opt in. And when food (or more accurately, starvation) is involved, it's also clear-cut. If the choice is between not eating at all, or working to eat, then both dogs and people will work. Love of work is no longer relevant; it's about survival.

The basic process for training dogs who don't want to work because they don't care about motivators and dogs who don't want to work because they want their motivators for free is the same. What's different is the frustration level on the part of the trainer. It's often extremely frustrating (and puzzling) when the dog clearly wants what you have but will not work for it. If this sounds like your dog, double check your training. Is what you're doing fun? Clear and easy to understand? Are you consistent? Do you avoid physical and emotional punishment? You need to go through the list of reasons why dogs appear low drive before you conclude your dog is the problem.

It's up to you to decide how hard or how long you are willing to squeeze your dog to get him to work against his will. If you decide that you are not willing to force your dog to work, then you accept that on any given day, you may or may not get work from your dog. If you decide that you want to do dog sports regardless of your dog's opinion, then you accept that you're making work a life or death proposition. No work means no food. At which point you have to ask yourself: Are you willing to work with a dog who truly does not want to work unless he feels that his survival depends on it?

No book or training technique can make your dog love to work or "fix" your dog. Temperament doesn't work like that. When a dad wants his son to play football and his son wants to play chess, you don't "fix" the child because there is nothing wrong with him! Not getting what you want does not mean there is something wrong with the other half - it just means that your interests are not aligned. This is the dog you have.

Can low drive dogs be trained for competition? Sure. Maybe. But you're going to need great training, a lot of patience, and a very accepting attitude when the dog decides it's not going to happen on that day. Further, lower working drive dogs will forever need a more attentive and engaged handler who makes a real effort to structure training sessions in an interesting and engaging fashion.

The High Drive Dog

Dogs with high working drive tend to have lower environmental attraction and can concentrate on work and training for long periods of time. It's very easy to overwhelm them with too much work early in their careers because they stay in the game well past the point that other dogs would opt out - even when tired, stressed, frustrated, or injured. If you show care and effort, they will work very hard for little reinforcement when they are mature. In fact, in some cases, the work IS the motivator because it taps into the dog's innate drives. Protection work, hunting, and herding are examples where the trial reality includes the reward of the work itself.

There are some enormous advantages to high working drive dogs. High drive dogs tend to come with a behavior package that includes good focus, trainability, persistence, and energy. They often manage to learn in spite of poor training. Very little time and attention needs to be spent developing motivators because high drive dogs bring a lot of natural interest in food and toys to the table. This is in sharp contrast to lower working drive dogs who benefit enormously from a systematic approach to building motivators.

Driven dogs can progress faster in training - but be careful! It's easy to push these dogs too hard, resulting in frustration behaviors like squeaking, whining, and anticipation errors in work. High drive dogs rarely walk away from a training session, but they will still express their distress in ways that you may prefer not to see! All dogs need sufficient rewards and deserve clarity in training. If your highly driven dog becomes frantic over errors in training or when asked for longer stretches of work without reinforcement, rethink your entire training plan. Slow down! Remember, driven dogs care very much about reinforcers, so withholding these things can be perceived as punishment when all the trainer was doing was trying to extend the time between rewards!

Highly Driven or Frantic?

Just as dogs are often labeled low drive when there are actually other issues at play, there are also dogs who are labeled high drive when they are nothing of the sort! Never mistake excessive movement for drive; stressed dogs often run (or "zoom") when they are overwhelmed. They are trying to reduce their stress and clear their heads with movement. This is not drive; it's frantic behavior! In fact, this is such a huge issue that an entire upcoming chapter is dedicated to it!

Strategies for Working with High Drive Dogs

<u>Strategic Proofing</u>

If you have a young, high drive dog, your focus needs to be on strategic proofing rather than reducing reinforcers. Because high drive dogs love to work, often for the sake of work itself, you're much better off helping your dog become stronger and more confident in his behaviors instead of extending the period of time your dog works to earn reinforcement. You want there to be no doubt in your dog's mind that he is performing correctly.

Here's an example: You have taught your dog to down quickly for a chance to play tug, which takes your dog two seconds to perform. While your first inclination might be to ask for several downs or position changes for one reward, rethink that plan! Strengthen the down behavior instead! Teach your dog to down when the toy is in your hand… on the ground… in your pocket… behind him... held by another person. Work the down behavior on all types of surfaces, from grass to cement to dirt. Be creative with your positioning; try facing away from him, sitting in a chair, or putting him behind a fence. All of these activities strengthen your dog's training, but none of them actually extend the period of time that your dog must function to get the reward.

Training in this fashion will allow your dog to retain a clear head, progress your training further, and allow you to move to longer stretches of work and behavior chains with fewer issues when your dog is mentally mature and ready for longer stretches of work.

Selecting Motivators

Some dogs care so much about the specific motivators used in training that they cannot think or process cues in their presence. For example, you cue "sit" and the dog just stares at you intently, possibly whining or barking, but definitely not sitting. Or the dog sits slo-o-o-owly, as if his rear end is on hydraulics. Although some handlers say these dogs have "too much drive," that's not really correct. The dog simply has not learned to think and work in the presence of specific motivators. This is particularly challenging when the dog learned a behavior for a lower value motivator and now the handler is asking the dog to do the same behaviors for a highly valued toy.

If your dog works fine for lower drive motivators, but cannot function when the big guns come out, then you need to teach him how. Start in a simple, non-distracting environment. Pull out a high value motivator and give a very simple cue that requires little to no processing. Behaviors using props such as a jump or a platform are ideal as there's really only one thing the dog might do in response to that prop. When your dog responds, reward instantly! This teaches your dog that you have no intention of withholding the motivator; when he realizes that he can count on it coming, his brain will settle down a bit. Then you can start adding cues that require a small amount of mental processing like a sit or down. Make it easy - we want him to be right - a lot!

When you add in chains of work - such as multiple jumps with weave poles, or anything that requires precision (like fronts) - set your dog up to be correct. For example, use a narrow platform so that your dog will be straight in front or put the guides on the weave poles. As your dog practices being right, he will improve his ability to function at a higher level of drive.

Ultimately, the answer to poor functioning in the presence of high value motivators is not to avoid using those motivators. Instead, train your dog with a lot of success in small increments and work your dog up to complex chains slowly so he learns that he can win no matter what is being asked in exchange.

Vocalization in High Drive Dogs

It is not uncommon for high drive dogs to become quite vocal when working. They usually do it as an unconscious expression of emotion, usually frustration. Dogs rarely go from frantic to thinking without some changes on your part, so do both of you a favor and make some changes as soon as you see the start of frustration rather than trying to wait the dog out.

One training change you can try is to reinforce your dog BEFORE the vocalization happens. If you miss your opportunity and your dog barks, feel free to bring your dog back to you, settle your dog however works best (for a high drive dog that might be a few high energy hand touches as opposed to cuddling), then go back to work. This time ask your dog to do a lot less to earn that reward.

Some trainers worry that doing this will create demand barking, so they are loathe to do anything that they think might be reinforcing the behavior. That's the wrong way to think of it.

Consider frustration as a stress response and take it from there. Most distress behaviors are not under the conscious control of the dog; the dog probably doesn't even know that the noises are leaking out! When dogs are distressed, they express it, so avoid the distress by rewarding your dog before it starts and watch the problem area disappear. Not convinced? Consider yourself for a moment. When you are frustrated that your computer won't start up and you call the help line, which is more likely to work for you - being told that you won't be helped until you calm down, or being told that someone is going to get to you right away and walk you through the steps to fix the problem?

Likewise, it's unlikely that you'll successfully teach your dog that vocalizing ends work or makes it shorter, even though that is a commonly used strategy. For example, some people might suggest that every time your dog starts to frustration bark while heeling, you should end the exercise and start all over again - with the end goal of communicating to your dog that barking makes him have to work twice as long to earn the reward. But if the dog is not conscious of the problem behavior (which he often isn't, since it's usually an unconscious frustration response), then making him conscious of it will take a good deal of energy away from what you want - following your cues. Here's a human example: When I am teaching a seminar, I tend to rock back and forth as I speak. I was unaware of this habit until I saw it on a video, at which point I realized that I move almost non-stop while teaching. Could I stop this behavior? Yes, but the energy it takes to remind myself not to move is so great that it distracts me from my ability to focus on my job. As soon as I get involved in what I am teaching again, the movement comes back. The longer I'm teaching without a break, and the more excited I get about my topic, the faster I move. If someone wanted to teach me not to move without ruining the quality of my presentation, they would have to control my excitement and give me more breaks rather than addressing the movement directly because movement is really only a symptom of the underlying issue.

The same is true for dogs. He could stop barking and whining if you communicated that you didn't like it, but the effort it would take would likely ruin his ability to work well and process your cues. And how are you going to make your dog aware of his behavior anyway? If you punish it, will your dog associate it with the noise he's making or with whatever cued behavior he was doing at that moment?

Working Drive and Competition Preparation

Before we wrap up this chapter, let's take a moment to consider how your dog's working drive might impact trial preparation.

There are two main methods of trial preparation: backchaining so that your dog expects a reward outside the ring, and making the ring and the work that takes place there the reward in itself. Both are valid methods, but the one you choose and the way you implement it will depend on your dog.

If you are working with a dog who truly works for the reward and who seems to take relatively little value from praise, play with the handler, or the actual exercises, then consider backchaining to a reward outside the ring. This is true for high or low drive dogs. However, if your dog has a lower working drive, back chain to the highest value reward you can. This gives the dog a reason to stay in the game. If your dog has higher working drive, focuses on classic rewards, and shows low frustration tolerance (a common combination), then consider backchaining to a relatively low value reward outside of the ring. This will work because the dog's drive will keep him in the game, while knowledge that the end reward is not hugely important will avoid the stress and frustration caused by wanting something very much.

If you have a dog who truly values working with you, then there's no need to back chain to a reward outside of the ring at all. In fact, doing so would lower the value of the interactive rewards provided in the competition ring. Teach your dog that rewards may or may not show up during working sessions. Sometimes you train with rewards and sometimes you do not. Just make sure that a high percentage of your training sessions do not involve rewards if you go this route!

For agility competitions, ALWAYS provide a high value reward outside the ring because the run is short, fast, and involves movement to release energy; the likelihood of building up frustration within the competition is very low.   It doesn't matter how strong the dog's drives are - the rewards are essential to lower drive dogs and a nice bonus to higher drive ones.

Obviously there are going to be dogs in between these extremes, and other dogs who take some value from the work but also appreciate some degree of back chaining to a reward outside the ring. Look at your dog, try out various options, and adjust accordingly. The purpose of this section is to help you find a starting point for competition preparation, but it's up to the handler to evaluate what works best and to make adjustments as needed. Train the dog you have!

Chapter Six

High Powered Dogs and Low Powered Dogs

Power is about the ability to get what you want. It has nothing to do with physical size, strength, or aggression; it is a quality of temperament and of the dog/handler match. A very tiny and assertive woman can have a good deal of power when paired with a cautious and soft natured 150 pound mastiff, while even the largest of men may find themselves at the mercy of a 12 pound terrier.

When it comes to power, the question is one of mental strength, the determination of each player to get what he or she wants, and each party's willingness to find alternatives when the direct route does not work. For this reason, when I talk about power dynamics, I am referring to two specific things. One is the amount of assertiveness and determination to "get one's way" in the specific dog (whether learned or innate), and the second is the relative amount of assertiveness of each party in the dog/human relationship in question.

Power dynamics tend to fall one of three ways: the high powered dog (and low powered human), the low powered dog (and high powered human), or a balanced pair where both the dog and the human have relatively similar amounts of power. In this chapter, we will look at each of these options, the issues each one brings to training, and ways to modify the amount of power that the dog has relative to his human.

By the way, it's important to note that dogs who are nervous cannot be accurately judged for elements of power, because nervous dogs are not expressing their temperament, they are expressing fear. For example, if you take your dog to a new place and he's climbing all over you and grabbing at your clothes, that is not a sign of high power. It's more likely that he's a frantic dog stressing up and looking for relief. If you see that behavior, calmly reassure your dog so he knows that you are connected and in control, then refer to the earlier chapter in this book on handling environmental discomfort.

High Powered Dogs

A dog with high levels of power is usually born with this predisposition. The power split can be such that the dog is totally in control. These dogs will bite their owners in order to get what they want; grab food, toys, or other objects with no regard for their trainer's personal space; and offer absolutely no cooperation or "give and take." Owners are often scared of these dogs - and rightfully so!

Some dogs are powerful and pushy right from the start. If they are allowed to take liberties early on, they just keep on taking them! After a while, it doesn't even occur to the dog not to take something if he wants it. This can start innocently enough; if a ten week old high-powered puppy bites his owner's hands in order to get the cookie in her fists, the owner will do one of two things. Either she will drop the cookie out of instinct or surprise, or she can move her hands out of reach. The high powered puppy in the first case will quickly learn that biting makes his owner drop food. When the owner begins to recognize the pattern, she might try holding on more tightly, but an innately persistent puppy will try biting harder and persisting longer. In the face of this escalation, the unsure owner might give up, dropping the food even faster to avoid the struggle (and the pain!). Soon, the owner is simply dropping whatever the puppy wants at the first sign of conflict.

This is a common scenario with children and dogs, with the result typically being that the child becomes afraid of the dog and the dog takes advantage of the situation. The dog is not aggressive; he is simply getting his way, using the methods that work for him. That same dog, in a relationship with another person, might show none of those behaviors because in that relationship those same behaviors have not worked for the dog. For example, while the children in a family might drop the cookie when the dog's mouth touches their hands, an adult might simply close their hand around the food, preventing access altogether.

A sophisticated owner might take it one step further, teaching the puppy that any attempts to take food without patiently waiting causes the hand to withdraw, until eventually the puppy learns what the trainer wishes to teach: wait patiently and you will be given what you want; try to take it and you will lose it every time.

Meanwhile, an experienced trainer might not only take the hand away, but also add penalty! Now the dog might have to do a series of behaviors to get that cookie or lose access altogether.

And while this may be a good option indeed for a high powered dog who needs to be recalibrated, it would be a very poor choice for a lower powered dog who isn't really asking for anything in the first place.

Low Powered Dogs

These dogs tend to be less pushy and determined by nature. They are innately unwilling to use any force to get their way and often prefer to look to a human for direction. These dogs tend to be sensitive by nature; if the owner's hand closes tightly around a cookie, they back off and try something different - or even just give up and walk away! Heck, the lowest powered dogs don't even think to ask in the first place!

Using the example from above, if a dog gently puts his teeth on a person to get a cookie and the owner accidentally dropped that cookie but then snatched it off the ground to prevent the puppy from getting it, a lower powered dog may interpret that as a strong correction. From that day forwards, the dog neither mouths the hands nor takes anything off the floor. Although this might sound desirable, that puppy would have actually benefitted from being allowed to get that cookie! Showing initiative (asking for the cookie by mouthing the hand) led to it being dropped so the puppy could have it. Having control over one's environment like this is a very important thing if you're trying to make a softer dog stronger.

At the extreme, I have seen dogs who have no power whatsoever. They quietly and passively follow all directions from the human leader exactly as directed. These dogs often behave with no energy, interactive drive, or initiative. They rarely look towards the handler and they ask for nothing (unless explicitly trained to do so). Sadly, this is exactly the type of behavior that many people want in their pet dogs.

If the dog's behavior is a result of the dog/handler power split more than an actual innate quality of the dog, the dog will likely show energy in life when AWAY from his handler.

The Relative Nature of Power

Although power can be innate, power dynamics are also relative - they are a function of two individuals: one dog and one person. The power split changes according to who the players are. The absolute levels of power are less important than the relative levels that each party brings to the table. Generally speaking, stronger people do better with dogs who are stronger by temperament. Softer dogs do better with softer handlers - or stronger handlers who know when to pull back their natural assertiveness and power so that the dog can feel stronger.

Power levels are neither good or bad - in dogs or in people. High powered people might get things done quickly because of their tendency to react quickly and with authority, but they might also do things wrong because they aren't thinking, leading to a higher error rate. The same is true with dogs. Meanwhile, lower powered people might be slower to react, but they also tend to think through their options and consider different angles more carefully. The same is true with dogs; a low powered dog is more likely to be precise, accurate, and show more care in his work.

The ideal situation is a power split where the dog is comfortable with his owner. The dog is confident about making decisions, respectful about waiting for food or toys, and clearly understands how to get what he wants. This dog is a team player! And the handler? Ideally she's leading the team, but with a sense of humor and benevolence! It's okay if the dog nudges her hand and gets a free cookie - occasionally. In fact, if it keeps a softer dog in the game, do it on purpose!

Problematic Power Dynamics

When the power dynamic between the dog and handler is off, specific patterns may emerge.

If the handler has too much power relative to her dog, you're likely to see a highly obedient, careful, and respectful dog. This may sound nice, but these dogs tend to move slower, even in response to cues. They are very careful not to invade the handler's space, which can be counterproductive when working on behaviors that require the dog to be close, like fronts and finishes. These dogs may check in frequently with the handler to make sure they're doing okay - but it's not from a positive place of "what are we going to do now?" Rather, it comes from a place of concern. These lower powered dogs also struggle with showing confidence when asked to make decisions; they are unlikely to show much initiative because they wait to be told what to do. These dogs often will not play with their handlers, either personally or with toys. In more extreme cases, you may see some very submissive behaviors in the presence of the handler such as a lowered head carriage, lip licking, submissive urinating and other classic signs of stress. They might even avoid the handler entirely if given the option.

On the other hand, if the handler has too little power when compared to the dog, the picture is quite different. It is common for the handler to lose control over training sessions. You may see low levels of natural obedience unless the dog can clearly see a reason to cooperate (food or toys in the handler's hand). The dog may move fast and impulsively, often angling to get what he wants (if a cookie hits the floor, the dog will be on it!). These dogs are less concerned about making mistakes, are often careless in their work, and they may try to steal reinforcement rather than earning it. There is often little regard for the handler's personal body or space. These dogs do not check in with their handlers unless they want something and they cannot see a direct route to getting it. Sometimes these dogs will use aggression to get their way by growling, posturing, or even biting!

Balanced teams are truly the best of both worlds. These dogs are aware of the handler's personal space, but confident about being close to the handler. They show eagerness for motivators but do not try to help themselves once they understand the basic rules of reinforcement (don't take things that have not been given to you and expect to put out some amount of effort in training to get what you want). Balanced dogs use the handler as a resource when unsure, but they do not do so excessively.

Power Issue or Impulse Control Problem?

Power issues are often confused with impulse control problems. How can you tell the difference?

When dogs have power, they CHOOSE their actions. They control what they do as a result of both their innate characteristics and life experiences, making their power both operant and trained. However, when dogs have impulse control issues, they are REACTING to their feelings; they do not control their emotions and the resulting actions. An impulsive dog might lunge for a cookie on the floor, not as a show of power, but because he is reacting to a feeling of desire. While the dog can learn self-control over time, there is nothing to be done once the dog has lost control except to get out of the situation.

As is true in most of training, the two issues can never be fully separated out, which is why I have an entire chapter coming up that is devoted to impulse control issues. However, you can begin to see the difference when you think about what happens when you have something that your dog really, really wants, like a new toy or a plate of delicious food.

High powered dogs will try to get that desirable item with consciously chosen behaviors. This might mean jumping on the handler to reach it or trying to knock it out of their handler's hands. Dogs who also have low impulse control will get MORE frantic over the next few seconds, quite possibly clawing, biting, and vocalizing - behaviors that are the result of emotional reaction, but that might still get them what they want. Dogs with both good impulse control and high power will either calm down and try to figure out how to get it, or they will get more determined, using whatever techniques have worked in the past.

It is important to note that determined is not the same as frantic. Determined means goal-focused, rational, and based on the dog's prior experiences. Frantic is simply noise, movement, and frustration, all of which often serves no purpose. Both can work for the dog, but one is a function of conscious thought (not an impulsive dog, but power) and the other is sheer luck (an impulsive dog who happened to throw out the right behavior at the right time).

Low powered dogs, on the other hand, are likely to stand a few feet back without making direct eye contact. They will not come in too close or make their interests clearly known, or, if they do, they will show appeasement behaviors such as lip licking, looking away, a low tail wag, and "groveling" in an effort to appease the human into giving it to them. They may behave in either a very calm fashion or show nervous excitement or conflict (circling, lowered head and body language, low level whining, or other signs of anxiety).

A dog with both low power and impulse control challenges is likely to behave erratically. The dog will possibly grovel (the conscious choice), but then try to jump up and get to the person's face or to the thing (the emotional reaction). Because the dog is jumping up, he can APPEAR to be a high powered dog, but high powered dogs don't grovel or show appeasement behaviors. It's the conflict between the conscious behavior and the emotional behaviors that shows that the dog is actually a low powered dog with an impulse control issue.

The more training your dog has when you consider this scenario, the more you will see the effects of training. That's good! Remember, what we care about is not the innate power of the dog *per se*. What we care about is how we are working with our dogs. For example, if your innately high powered dog immediately offers a polite sit and eye contact when you have something desirable, that's awesome! And if your innately low powered dog jumps on you or grabs for the thing because you have trained pushy behavior to build confidence, then that's also awesome!

It's worth taking a moment to think about how you would

respond in this scenario. If you would find yourself feeling nervous at the thought of holding something that your dog might really want, you might be a lower powered human with a higher powered dog. On the other hand, if you said "no" and your dog shut down completely, it's likely that you are a high powered human with a lower powered dog. And if you would expect cooperation from your dog and would be willing to wait calmly to get it, you're probably fairly evenly matched. It's not good or bad; it's all a matter of balance and considering where you are at today.

Changing Power Dynamics

The goal of "power work" is to bring the dog and the handler to a closer state of balance. Remember that you'll need to change your expectations over time as both of you change in response to life experiences; constantly reevaluate your situation!

Using Personal Pressure

Power can be changed in subtle ways, and using personal pressure wisely is one of the easiest ways to do so. Pressure is not good or bad; it just is. If you understand it, you can make educated choices about whether you want to add or reduce pressure for your dog at any given moment. As a general rule, we add pressure to powerful dogs and release it for more fragile ones. Here are some factors you can take into consideration when working with your dog:

- Your direction of travel. Moving towards your dog adds pressure. Backing up or turning away releases it. This is true with play as well; dragging a dog behind you with a toy reduces pressure, as does allowing a dog to follow you from behind.

- Direction you are facing. The more you face your dog, the more pressure you are applying. On the other hand, the back of your body is total pressure reduction; you're perceived as escaping prey!

- Your expression. Staring (a non-smiling expression with continuous eye contact) pressures your dog; staring quietly at your dog may cause him to wonder if you are unhappy. An open, happy, smiling, laughing, and talking human face is inviting, which lowers the amount of pressure on your dog.

- Your voice. An engaged and supportive voice suggests you are enjoying the current interaction, whereas an intense voice is another form of pressure, even if you're happy! For example, if your dog is distracted by the world and you use a forceful voice and behavior to "jolly" your dog, that is enormous pressure to your dog!

- Eye contact. Direct eye contact is pressure. Looking away or at the ground releases it. Fragile dogs can be taught to enjoy direct eye contact, but it is likely to take some effort. Combine eye contact with a nice smile and some verbal interaction to make this easier for your lower powered dog.

- Play behavior. Imitating a dog's natural play movements reduces pressure. If your dog offers you a play bow and you offer one back, that is pressure reduction. You have "accepted" his offer to play. But if you ask your dog to play, and your dog does not engage, yet you continue to try to play anyway, you're increasing pressure.

Raising Your Dog's Power

Choice is critical for all dogs, but especially for low powered dogs. Allow your dog to have maximum choice in his life. Don't get upset with your dog if he accidentally bites your hands when playing or taking a toy. Let him jump on you, demand bark, and otherwise behave in a slightly obnoxious manner. Obviously, you always have to choose the "misbehaviors" that you are comfortable with, but be aware that your choices will have consequences. If these behaviors become an annoyance, it's time to reevaluate your dog; maybe he isn't so low power after all!

There are two exercises that I find to be excellent in helping to raise a dog's power.

The first is "place" which is what I call the position between my legs. You can teach a dog to stay in "place" simply by feeding him there continuously as you move around. After a while, try moving without the lure - most dogs will stay there! Reward generously.

Once a dog is fluent at place, make it a tiny bit harder for your dog to get there by bringing your legs closer together so your dog has to push into this space. This is a great way to teach your dog that it is okay to be pushy with you and to make it clear that you welcome contact with your body. Note: do not move your feet together after the dog is in position - that is threatening. Place your feet where you want them and then bring the dog into position.

The second exercise is using a platform. Because dogs who have been trained with platforms tend to love them (they get lots of cookies up there!), you can use this to your advantage. Your goal is to get closer and closer to your dog. For example, if your dog doesn't like you close when in front of you, then place the platform in front of you. Now, slowly, work your way into your dog's personal space, just an inch at a time. You can eventually include looming over your dog and feeding through your legs. You might even walk over your dog so his head is between your legs or behind you; this will help desensitize your dog to the pressure of your body.

Lowering Your Dog's Power

If you need to lower your dog's power, face your dog with the front of your body or move forwards into his space to get his attention. Calm your body and your voice and EXPECT cooperation! Don't respond to your dog's intensely pushy behaviors. Project leadership and, if needed, practice impulse control exercises. Your dog can and will learn to offer cooperation to get his needs or desires met.

You can also use a platform to lower your dog's power. To do this, place your platform away from you, but keep the toys or treats in your hands or pockets. In order to get reinforced, your dog will need to move away from you - out of your personal space. When you're ready to reward him, take the treat to him; if he gets off the platform, stop walking towards him. Stay calm. Your body movement tells your dog if he's correct or not. The goal is for the dog to learn that mugging the handler or coming in for a treat ends the handler's decision to move towards the dog.

Don't Forget...

What you want to remember about power is that it's not good or bad; it's a relative quality that will influence how your dog behaves and works under a variety of circumstances. It is being endlessly affected by each of your daily interactions, second by second. Your job is to develop an understanding of how your power compares to your dog's, and then take steps to raise, lower, or maintain your basic power dynamic according to what makes the most sense for your team.

Chapter Seven

Biddable, Handler Sensitive and Handler Hard Dogs

 Handler sensitivity and biddability refer to the extent to which your dog wants to please you and avoids displeasing you. If you call your dog - and you know that he heard you - does he look at you and then walk away? Is his response dependent on whether or not you have a cookie in your pocket - and a good one at that? Or does he act more like a puppet on a string, cooperating even when it appears that he does not want to? Assuming that your dog has received excellent quality training and understands what you've asked him to do, his response to this scenario will tell you a lot about his basic biddability and handler sensitivity.

Biddability

Biddability is the degree to which a given dog wants to cooperate with his handler and keep him happy. Boiled down to the simplest description, a biddable dog is a team player. These dogs work hard to get you to interact with them, and they thrive on your personal time together. They tend to be good-natured and cooperative. They may have many interests, but they are happiest when you are happy. This is a very desirable quality in a performance dog; indeed, there is no downside.

Training Biddable Dogs

Biddable dogs are a gem for performance trainers! To maintain this quality, go ahead and start training early and often; you want your dog to develop a love of work and interaction with you. If you want to use a no reward marker (NRM) in training (I avoid them), these dogs will generally tolerate it very well. Be careful not to use food and toys when they're not needed, such as in general life lessons - there's no reason to use a cookie for a dog who is thrilled to work for praise and personal approval! Reserve classic motivators for your precision work!

Handler Sensitivity

Whereas the biddable dog works to keep you happy, the handler sensitive dog is trying to prevent you from becoming unhappy. This may seem like the same thing, but the truth is, a handler sensitive dog may not care that much if you are pleased, smiling, and warm with him. However, he will care very much if he thinks you are angry or unhappy with him.

Handler sensitivity can make training much more complicated because these dogs are worriers. "Are you unhappy now? How about now? And now??!!" Rather than focusing on the job at hand, they seem to fret about their handler's reactions.

While the general use of the word "biddable" in regards to dogs always has a positive connotation, the term "handler sensitivity" has both a positive and a negative connotation. On the one hand, it's considered positive because the dog will work hard to avoid unhappiness in the relationship with the handler. On the other hand, these dogs shut down easily if they think the handler is displeased. In other words, it's biddability taken to an extreme. These dogs can be TOO sensitive, and if they are paired with a handler with little frustration tolerance, it can be disastrous. They care about every real (or imagined) bit of unhappiness from the handler. Emotional pressure is very real to these dogs, even if they have never experienced any direct physical harm or threat of harm.

When a biddable but not excessively handler sensitive dog makes an error and does not earn reinforcement, he simply tries again, changing his behavior to be more in line with what the handler wants (assuming he can figure it out). In the same situation, the handler sensitive dog is just as likely to experience excessive stress, which actually impedes his ability to change behavior. Instead, he might attempt to leave training, shut down, or become frantic.

Depending on the dog's overall tendency, handler sensitivity will be expressed as either stressing up or stressing down. Handler sensitive dogs who stress up may vocalize, jump at the trainer's face, pant a lot, "climb" up the handler, or lick the handler with quick, nervous licks. Handler sensitive dogs who stress down may behave very differently, moving very little, showing slow reactions to cues, appearing shut down and distressed, or leaving training altogether.

Handler sensitivity is neither good nor bad - if it is not extreme. On the plus side, handler sensitive dogs will try to work for us, even when they know there is little or nothing in it for them, just to maintain a happy status quo with their handler. This is excellent for trialing! They might not be truly happy about working and they may not be flashy to watch, but they won't opt out if they know what they need to do. On the negative side, dogs with more extreme sensitivity can be hard to train and struggle in sports, especially if their chance of making a mistake is high, or if the handler doesn't (or can't) give clear direction. In agility, they tend to be cautious and slow. In obedience, they tend to struggle in higher-level classes, wondering if they have made good choices. If the handler fails to interact with them in a "normal" fashion in competition, they shut down very easily, which can ruin any chance of a high quality performance.

Puppies are not normally biddable or handler sensitive; these qualities usually develop over time and are a function of relationship and how the dog is raised and trained - though no doubt there is a very strong genetic component. My experience is that the more you train a given dog with relationship-based, positive reinforcement methods and a liberal use of personality and warmth in your interactions, the more biddability and handler sensitivity you'll begin to see. And the reverse can also be true; some dogs respond to compulsion training by tuning out their handlers unless they have immediate concerns about how it might affect them personally.

Training Handler Sensitive Dogs

Handler sensitive dogs should be trained at their pace. Work slowly and carefully and ensure that each step of a new behavior is well understood before adding additional steps. Splitting behaviors to their component parts is critical; these dogs do not tolerate lumping in the learning process! Furthermore, do not create behavior chains until each foundation behavior is solid. As much as possible, strive for errorless learning environments.

Use reinforcement generously. When errors occur, consider rewarding your dog and ending the training session. This allows you to rethink your training plan while minimizing the stress on your dog. Do not express your negative emotions or frustrations in training because your dog will get stressed. If your dog does begin to stress, end the session with a free reinforcer and give your training plan some more thought.

When preparing for competition, work hard to ensure that your dog recognizes that the ring environment is safe (prepare for that!) and that silence means that all is well. Handler sensitive dogs have a very high need for emotional support and they will look to you often to see how they should respond to possible threats in the environment. When competing with these dogs, you need to remain calm, confident, and collected so that the dog can function.

<u>Handler Hard Dogs</u>

At the other end of the spectrum, we have handler hard dogs. Handler hard dogs don't worry about making errors. The cookies, the toys, and the work itself are far more important to the dog than the relationship and interaction with the handler. These dogs can be easier to train because they handle mistakes well without getting upset or losing their ability to think clearly; they simply try again to gain reinforcement.

Handler hard dogs can be excellent competitors because they are not likely to be bothered by their handler's stress during competition or the errors that are bound to happen there. On the other hand, they are much more likely to opt out of work when the reinforcers are gone. It often appears that it's all about what's in it for them, not maintaining a positive status quo with the handler.

Handler hardness can be a function of genetics as some dogs are just born more independent and self sufficient, but it can also be created by handlers who make no effort to include relationship and warm interactions in their training. Indeed, the quickest way to create handler hardness in a genetically independent dog is a combination of punishment and a detached demeanor. The dog quickly develops very self-interested behavior rather than cooperation.

Training Handler Hard Dogs

These dogs often benefit from a more structured lifestyle. For example, instead of simply opening the door when the dog asks to go outside, ask him to sit first!

Handler hard dogs can be trained a lot of ways - as long as they see what's in it for them. You would do well to include as much personality in your training as possible to build your dog's love of personal interactions, even when it seems like you're wasting your time. Generally emphasize handler control and more direction in the training program. While all dogs love having choice, these dogs do not need choice to build their confidence.

Be aware that although these dogs often appear to do very well when trained with compulsion, compulsion actually builds handler hardness. These dogs quickly figure out when you can't punish them (like in the ring at a trial) and therefore may fail to perform in those contexts. It's much better to put your energy into teaching your dog that cooperation and internal controls will satisfy their interests.

During trial preparation, you'll need to be especially careful to ensure your dog understands the path to reinforcement.

If you choose to back chain to a classic reward outside of the competition environment, take your time so it is abundantly clear to the dog that his work in one space is what causes the reward at the end of training.

It's a Spectrum

As in most things, dogs are not all one or all the other. Biddability and handler sensitivity are on a spectrum. In addition, behavior is often contextual. A dog may be more handler sensitive in one context than in another. For example, dogs are often more sensitive and biddable in agility training where the dog has had more positive training, as compared to obedience, where the dog may have been trained with more traditional methods. In the same dog, different aspects of the dog's temperament have been developed and expressed.

It's also important to understand that a dog who starts handler hard can develop sensitivity and biddability through experience. My dog Cisu was genetically handler hard, but training and time brought about her biddability and handler sensitivity as she developed a love of the work and interaction with me. Therefore, start your training where your dog is right now, but be ready to change your approach as your dog changes as well!

Chapter Eight

Impulse Control and Self-Control

The phrase "impulse control" is often heard in both dog and human circles, and with good reason! The inability of both humans and dogs alike to control our desires is one of the biggest sources of unhappiness in our lives.

Consider these examples: Some humans cannot control their impulse to eat unhealthy - yet tasty! - foods, and as a result gain undesirable amounts of weight and develop health conditions that are directly related to a lack of self-control. Some humans cannot control their impulse to spend money, creating enormous amounts of debt, which adds considerably to the stress of daily living. Some humans cannot control their impulse to express their opinions, leading to hurt feelings, arguments, and resentment among friends, loved ones, and co-workers. Some humans cannot control their sexual impulses, leading to feelings of personal guilt and broken families when their indiscretions are discovered.

In the vast majority of cases we are "sorry" about our choices. We wish we hadn't eaten that piece of cake, ran up our credit card bills, spoken out of turn, or engaged in an affair that ended our marriage. Yet we do not seem to learn. We do not change our behavior, even when faced with very similar circumstances. How is it possible that we repeatedly make choices that do not serve us well, even when we are well aware of the negative consequences and bad feelings that we are likely to experience later? Why don't we simply change our behavior so that we can reap the long-term benefits?

And why do we expect our dogs to be able to do what we cannot?

Impulse Control vs. Self-Control

While these terms are normally used interchangeably, I will differentiate them for this chapter in order to separate out those choices that we can influence with our dogs (self-control) and those that we cannot (impulse control).

Impulse control issues result from either a reflex (such as a startle) or from being over threshold (being so upset or excited that the dog cannot make a conscious choice). In both cases, the dog does not make a choice about how he reacts. He just does. Impulse control issues are not responsive to training.

Self-control issues result from conscious decision making; the dog decides whether or not to act. Therefore, we can influence a dog's level of self-control through training.

Although we often say that a dog has an impulse control problem, what we really mean is that the dog has a self-control problem. For example, if you hold up your plate and your dog knocks it out of your hands and eats the food, then your dog has learned, rationally, that he can be rewarded for bad behavior. Although this is not an impulse control problem because the dog made a conscious choice, it is a training problem, and it definitely needs to be addressed.

Regardless of how much we like to believe that we are always making choices rationally, the reality is that both people and dogs often do things without thinking; we react impulsively and without any thought at all. Impulse control challenges come from the dog's inability to weigh the pluses and minuses - the dog reacts without thinking.

At the end of the day, a dog with a training problem may look identical to a dog with an impulse control problem, but they are not the same. It's critically important to understand if the problem your dog is struggling with is an impulse control problem or a self-control problem because training assumes a rational participant who is capable of making conscious choices about his behavior. If your dog reacts without thought - impulsively - then any consequences applied after the fact will not work.

To make things more complicated, when we're training, the dog is flipping back and forth between these two possibilities, especially in high-intensity training like bite work or if the dog is high drive and obsessive about the motivators being used. This is especially true of dogs who are working near their threshold; one moment they are thinking and aware, and then they are not. This typically results in behavior that spirals higher and higher out of control.

Here's a human example of an impulsive response. Let's say you were alone in a room when someone quietly entered through the door behind you. You didn't hear them enter, so when you turned around and saw them, you were startled and screamed. The other person didn't appreciate your scream, so you got smacked on the head - which hurt! What happens the next time someone comes into the room unnoticed by you? Chances are you will still startle and utter a scream. In both cases, you didn't actually choose to scream in the first place; it happened reflexively.

To make a human less likely to startle and scream, we'd need to make some changes. We could encourage the person to sit facing the door - if they see someone else come in, there is no reason to startle and therefore no reason to scream. We could make them aware of the fact that people frequently come and go, so they can begin to expect this change in the environment, which would again reduce the likelihood that they would startle and scream. No matter how you approach the problem, the first step is to make the person conscious of what is happening so that they are not caught off guard. We want them in the "deciding" part of their brain, not the "reacting" part.

The same is true with dogs. To handle truly impulsive behavior - as opposed to issues of self-control - we need to make our dog aware and thoughtful about what's going on. This allows him to move from impulsive reactions to rational self-control. Doing this requires us to first control the environment, and then to set up many training opportunities so that the dog can become familiar with what might happen in that place. Remember, it's not about whether or not the dog WANTS to cooperate, it's about whether or not he CAN cooperate. Once the dog is aware and thinking, we can begin a training plan that allows the dog to make choices.

The important point here is that you can only train a rational and thinking animal, and impulsive animals are neither rational nor thinking.

The Role of Maturity on Impulsive Behavior

Although we can improve our dog's impulsive tendencies with our training choices, we need to remember that there are biological realities that affect our dog's ability to make the types of choices that we like to see. Age makes a tremendous difference on a dog's ability for exercising self-control - just as it does in people! And just like with people, some will become extremely good at it while others never seem to make much progress at all. The amount of training we need to invest will vary greatly based on our dog's innate tendencies in this area.

For those who are young and learning, management is truly your best friend! When we are young, our parents structure our choices to prevent too many misfortunes. Rather than attempting to teach young children not to eat ALL of the cookies in the box, we simply bring out the number we are willing to give them and put the rest away. We ignore any pleas for more cookies lest we "train" our children to be demanding to get what they want.

The doggy equivalent is obvious. Just because your six-month-old puppy is almost full sized on the outside doesn't mean that he is mentally mature; you cannot use what you can see (physical size) to gauge what you cannot (mental maturity). Instead, set up environments that focus on management to prevent bad habits while you develop a training plan that also increases your dog's capacity for self-control.

Teaching Self-Control

Teaching self-control requires some work on your part, but the end result is definitely worth it. The basic process is to ensure you have environmental control, make your dog aware of something he wants, and then teach him what he should do under those circumstances.

Start by being sure that you have environmental control. If you're trying to teach your dog to exercise self-control when there are cookies on the ground, but your dog is finding and eating crumbs you don't know about, your training will be pointless. Vacuum if you must! Environmental control can be tedious, but it is critical to your success.

The next step, making your dog aware of the item he wants, is key. Just like the person who is constantly aware that a new person might walk in the room will not unconsciously startle and scream, when your dog is constantly aware of distractions – like food on the ground - he can then learn to exercise self-control. If you try to prevent your dog from noticing the distraction, you increase the likelihood that he'll have an impulsive reaction - and you can't train a dog who isn't thinking!

Sometimes handlers go catatonic when they see distractions in the environment, which basically frees the dog to do as he wishes since he hasn't been given anything else to do. Other handlers take it the opposite direction; they see distractions and they become intense and hysterical in an effort to keep the dog with them and unaware of the alternatives. Neither makes sense. Your dog needs to be aware of what is out there, and then he needs to know what he should be doing instead.

Finally, you'll teach a behavior that is incompatible with lunging for the distraction. For example, a dog cannot eat a cookie from the floor while heeling, doing a recall, sitting and staying, doing agility contacts… the list is endless! To make this work, you must make the behaviors requested reasonable and fast paced, and you must hold the dog to criteria. If the dog is struggling, you either need to change to easier exercises, get further away from the distraction, or raise your rate of reinforcement. Regardless, make sure that there is something clear cut for your dog to do.

Be sure that when you're working with your dog you stay engaged! If the work is going to stop for any reason (to move equipment, set up for a new exercise, etc.) consider what you do with your dog at that time. If you know that you are in a high distraction situation, don't leave this time to chance; structure your dog! Place your dog in a crate, on a down stay, or on a mat (assuming he is comfortable with those options). If you are extremely confident that your dog will not leave you during work to grab a distraction, you can set your dog free when you're not working. Allow him to explore - and quite possibly eat - the distractions on the floor. For some dogs this works just fine as a form of Premack. However, if you do this and find that it increases your dog's level of distractibility, stop doing it and go back to structuring your dog's break time.

To make this abstract concept a bit more concrete, let's walk through this process using the behavior of "scarfing food off the floor in the training room." This is an incredibly common problem: you're walking along with your dog and before you know what happened, your dog smells a cookie on the floor and snags it! Odds are good that this is a reflexive behavior; dog smells cookie and cookie is eaten. In addition it is learned; your dog knows from past experiences that cookies are probably on that floor.

The first step is to control the environment to prevent him from reacting reflexively, so you are going to start with a pristine training area and prepare some cookies in advance. In order to prevent him from eating any cookies and self-reinforcing, you're going get some pieces of paper that are roughly the same size, shape, and color as bits of food and store them in a baggie to increase the association. Bits of rolled up paper towels work well.

Now you want to make your dog aware of the "cookie" distraction, so drop a few pieces of paper bits on the floor while he is watching. Make sure that he sees what you're doing, but don't allow him to be so close that he can reach those pieces of paper! Have him tied, in a crate, or held by someone else if you need to. Ideally, he will be so far away from the distraction that he'll be interested in what you've dropped, but not dive-bombing towards it. If he does, he's too close. Move further away.

If he is staring at the "cookie" (paper) and shows no signs of acknowledging you, wait him out. Once he finally turns back to you, give him a real cookie from your hand. Move towards another paper "cookie" and repeat. Continue doing this until your dog glances at the paper and then looks to you.

At this point, he has shown that he is making a conscious choice, which means he's in a trainable place. Now we'll add in an incompatible behavior; heeling or loose leash walking works very well for this scenario. Starting far enough away that he can do his job, move past the "cookie" distraction. You will now reward him for work, not for ignoring the distraction.

As he masters this exercise, you can increase the challenge level. Here are some ideas: Take those same pieces of paper but this time add food to the bag to create food scented pieces of paper. Drop only paper. Then drop actual food. Try placing food in covered containers (like plastic containers with holes poked in them or food bowls covered with women's stockings so he can't reward himself) and move past those. Work off leash – but be sure you can control his access to the food, so consider having a helper. If you'd like more details on how to approach teaching your dog to work through distractions, pick up a copy of my book *Beyond the Back Yard: Train Your Dog to Listen Anytime, Anywhere!*

As you work through this process, you can choose to reward from your hand, or you can go pick up the distraction food from the floor to give your dog, or (if your dog isn't impulsive), you can give him permission to go back to the distraction for the reward. When you choose how to reward, keep your dog in mind. For dogs who really struggle with impulsive behavior, it's probably best for the handler to go get the food and bring it to the dog because that keeps the dog in a more controlled state. Impulsive dogs often need that sense of handler control to keep them thinking about making good choices.

This type of work is stressful for your dog because he has to work hard to focus, so keep the distraction training sessions short, and work hard to make the challenges attainable. When you want to relax and work on training behaviors, select environments where you know self-reinforcement is not possible (a freshly vacuumed training space, on leash work, or train in your own house or yard where no food has been dropped).

This process isn't easy. It requires selecting the right level of challenges, and trainers tend to get carried away. They want to start with hot dogs on the floor right under their dog's nose, and then do a recall over the top of it. That won't work. You need to start with a piece of paper 10 feet away, and then do a much simpler behavior and reward generously. You need to prevent the dog from self-reinforcing. And in the work, you need to give the dog something to do - and ensure that you stay very connected with your dog.

Should You Work on Self-Control with Your Dog?

This may seem like an odd question, but if your dog is soft, tentative, and not terribly interested in what you have to offer, I'd suggest skipping self-control exercises altogether, at least initially. For one thing, these types of dogs often aren't very impulsive. For another, self-control is often directly contradicted by drive building, which is what these softer dogs tend to need. In drive building, we work to build the dog's love of the "thing" and to do so, we apply external controls such as using a leash to hold the dog back and encouraging our dogs to actively resist and pull forward.

If, over time, you notice that your wallflower dog is becoming bolder and more self-assured, it might be time to introduce self-control exercises then. But the fact is that well trained, tentative dogs don't usually think to run off and grab things off the floor because they are trying to be good - and "being good" (assuming the dog is trained to understand the behaviors that he is performing) does not include leaving work for free snacks.

Give Your Dog a Break

While trainers often find it quite frustrating when dogs fail to control themselves, it's only fair to point out that we humans struggle mightily with these issues as well, so let's give our dogs a break and focus on what we can control - our training choices.

Chapter Nine

Understanding Movement

Why do humans move? For the same reasons that dogs move! Because we're nervous, or excited, or energetic by nature, or simply because we like to use our bodies!

And why do we stop moving? Because we're tired, or sick, or thinking hard, or scared, or getting ready to spring into action!

The fact that our dog is moving tells us relatively little about our dog's motivations. To understand movement, we first need to understand the reasons that dogs move in general. Then, we need a baseline understanding of what is normal for our particular dog. Without this contextual information, simply noting that a dog is moving (or not) is meaningless.

Working Drive

Dogs who are bred for work or dog sports often love to move, whether that is through play, work, or exercise. Dogs with high levels of working drive frequently show high levels of energy as their normal baseline. They are not content to simply sit on the couch. They like to be busy, and often their brains are spinning just as fast as their bodies! If you don't give these dogs things to do, they will find things to do - usually at your expense.

These dogs also tend to get excited easily. Got a tasty morsel or a ball in your hand? These dogs see it and quickly ratchet their energy up! This is a normal response for driven dogs who want something, and while it might pair with impulse control challenges, in and of itself the movement is of no concern.

High levels of movement are simply normal parts of their temperamental package, so when they show that quality in training, it's much less telling of their emotional states than it might be for a different type of dog. What you need to look for is whether that movement is focused or not. Dogs with a lot of working drive show focused energy; it's easy to tell WHY they are behaving in an energetic fashion. For example, if there is a ball stuck under a couch in the room, the high drive dog will not run around wildly. Instead, he will focus his physical and mental efforts on getting to that ball. If your high drive dog is moving wildly but you cannot identify a reason for that movement, you are probably seeing stress rather than enthusiasm.

Some dogs are not particularly driven, but still move a lot. This can be normal; some breeds (in general) and individuals (in particular) love to run for the sake of running. While this might also be called "zooming," the difference from frantic, stress-based zooming is that there is nothing else going on. The dog isn't trying to escape from anything, and he's just as likely to zoom around the back yard as anywhere else. He thinks running is fun!

If you have a dog who likes to move a lot, you will need to do something! Take that energy and channel it into work. Use the ball stuck under the couch to reward your dog's great work. Make sure that your dog gets plenty of physical and mental exercise, both of which can be satisfied by training for competition sports. And that dog who loves to run simply to run? Go ahead and channel as much of that as possible into work - it might be a fantastic motivator for your dog.

Stress-Related Movement

When dogs who are not normally energetic start to show high levels of movement, it's worth taking a moment to figure out what is causing that behavior.

Start by determining where your dog's focal point is. If your dog is moving wildly around a new space but without any particular focus, then your dog's movement is being generated by nervousness. In human terms, your dog is pacing; he's trying to soothe himself into a better place mentally by moving his body. Next, examine if anything in particular happened immediately before he started showing high levels of energy. Even a simple No Reward Marker (NRM) can send sensitive dogs zooming wildly away. Finally, look at what else your dog is doing. Signs that he might be feeling stressed include leaving wet footprints on the ground, panting heavily, and lunging at other dogs or people.

If your dog "stresses up" in new places, don't channel that energy into work, even if your dog shows a lot of working drive. Instead, work to calm your dog's mental state before you begin training. Training frantic dogs is a bad idea for several reasons, but the main one is that these dogs tend to be mentally scattered, which means that they will struggle to accurately follow your cues. That leads to a dynamic where your dog is likely to make a lot of errors, and frantic dogs who make errors have a tendency to get worse. If you've ever seen a dog make an error in an agility trial and then start to run around frantically (zooming), you've seen this in action.

Even frantic dogs who never zoom are poor candidates for training because it's easy for them to associate stress and nervousness with work. That's no good. While there is never a reason to encourage your dog to be catatonic before you train him, work to differentiate a positive form of movement and energy (let's do something!) from movement and energy which is generated from distress (I'm overwhelmed!).

Self-Control or Stress?

It's fairly common to hear people talk about self-control exercises for dogs who are zooming, but that only makes sense if the dog has a self-control issue. Most zooming is a stress response, not a self-control problem.

If you aren't sure if your dog has a stress problem or a self-control problem, consider this. Dogs with self-control issues start out under control, see something that they want, and then leave that place of control to run TOWARDS the desired thing. Dogs who are zooming due to stress will also start out under control, but have no particular focal point when they lose control. The primary difference is the point at which the dog decides to go towards something. In other words, if the dog leaves training because of something attractive out there, the issue is self-control. If zooming or extreme movement is after the dog has left the training situation, then the issue is stress, and the desired thing is simply something that coincidentally crossed the dog's path. And as often as not, it's a bit of both.

Here are some examples:

Archer - Lack of Self-Control

Archer enters the agility field on leash, reasonably focused and contained. The leash is removed and the dog placed on a stay. The handler knows that her dog is prone to running off, so as she walks away backwards, she holds up her hand and repeatedly chants, "Stay, stay, stay." When she's about 15 feet away, Archer looks over to the left and spies a dog standing near the field. His ears perk up and he takes off, running directly to the other dog. Archer starts to greet the other dog but then remembers that he was supposed to be sitting on a start line. Rather than returning to his handler, though, he simply starts running all over the place.

This dog shows a classic self-control issue; he sees a dog and can't help himself so he runs off to visit. However, after a brief greeting, he realizes he's in trouble, so now he switches from a self-control problem to a stress problem, so he keeps going. Or maybe he has no stress at all, but now that he's free and zipping around, he sees no reason to return and plenty to do in the meantime - lack of self-control that has run amuck.

The solution is self-control training. The handler needs to control the environment (primarily with distance) and slowly add expectations as the dog shows readiness. The dog needs to be aware of what is out there in the training set-ups so he can make a conscious choice. This dog should not go to a trial until he has demonstrated, in training, that he can manage his behavior in situations even more challenging than he is likely to see at the dog show. If this dog is also sensitive by temperament, his handler will need to keep an eye on his stress levels as well.

Bruno - Lack of Confidence

After Bruno enters the agility field, his handler removes the leash. Just like Archer, Bruno is prone to breaking his stay, so the handler walks away backwards, holding up her hand and repeatedly chanting, "Stay, stay, stay." As the handler moves further away, Bruno's ears go back flat on his head and his eyes get wider. He starts to lick his lips and breaks eye contact with his handler. He stands up and takes a few tentative steps towards the first obstacle without being cued. His handler attempts to save the situation by starting to run the course and cuing the first obstacle, but it's too late; Bruno veers away and runs off. After a few feet, Bruno sees another dog on the side of the field. He runs directly to the other dog, and when he gets there, he starts to greet the dog intensely and nervously. Then he's off again, his mouth wide open, his ears pinned back, frantically running from dog to dog, person to person, and becoming very hard to catch.

Although the two situations may seem similar, they are actually quite different. This is classic zooming caused by stress. The solution is to reduce the dog's stress at the agility field. Bruno's handler needs to deal with the root behavior issue and refrain from trialing until he is confident and ready to be there. Every time a stressed dog is left on the start line and manages his stress by zooming, future changes become much harder to make for the dog and handler alike.

Cairo - Lack of Engagement

Once again, the situation is familiar. Cairo enters the agility field pulling on leash and looking around. The leash is removed, and because Cairo's handler knows that he's prone to breaking his stay, she walks away backwards, holding up her hand and repeatedly chanting, "Stay, stay, stay." As the handler moves further away, Cairo looks around. He sees a dog and watches for a few seconds. Deciding that he'd rather go visit than play agility, he runs off to see the other dog. After a quick greeting, he notices a training bag on the ground and he sticks his nose in to see if there are any treats. There are none, so he travels a few feet to the side where a child is sitting in a chair eating a cookie and he tries to grab it. Cairo then finds a few more cookies on the ground, eats them, and when he can't find anything else to eat or dogs to visit, he cheerfully runs back to his owner, ready to play the agility game.

This dog needs self-control training, but the handler also needs to work hard to either improve the dog's love of the sport or develop their mutual engagement. Cairo does not appear to be stressed, nor particularly sensitive. The fact that he made a clear choice to leave the work without signs of stress suggests that the dog was never engaged in the first place. If you're seeing this in a trial, it's likely that you are also seeing it in training. Make changes to develop your engagement in work!

These examples should illustrate that self-control training won't solve the problem of zooming in training because zooming is a stress problem rather than one of self-control. Of course, some dogs have both; they are stressed dogs who also suffer for lack of self-control. But those are still two different issues that need to be addressed separately because they have two different solutions. Indeed, training for a self-control problem when it's actually a stress problem is likely to make the stress worse because self-control training adds measured quantities of stress by asking the dog to make difficult decisions.

Of course, there's always an exception to the rule. A lot of self-control issues do have an element of stress associated with them. For example, the dog KNOWS that you do not want him to disengage to steal food, visit people, or grab a toy but he can't quite help himself. So what started out as a simple engagement or impulse control issue is now an engagement or impulse control issue with major stress attached to it, and they feed off each other. Which means that after your dog does the bad thing, he becomes stressed, so he zooms rather than returning to the handler. And since a zooming dog is at a high risk for poor decision making, you may also see your zooming dog start to grab random stuff as he runs - because he's now having a first class meltdown. So many problems, all at one time!

It's important to get a handle on each element. When in doubt, assume it's stress and treat it as such. While treating an engagement or impulse control issue like a stress issue won't make the dog worse, it also won't make him better. The reverse is not true. Treating a stressed dog like a dog with self-control problems can make him worse, so tread more carefully there.

The Bottom Line

When it comes to movement, you need to understand what is motivating your dog's movement and then learn all you can about addressing each type of movement. If it's simply an enthusiastic and joyful response to a change, then give the dog something to do! If the issue is stress, refer back to the chapter that addresses nervous dogs, and if the issue is one of impulse control, refer to that one. Finally, if the issue is lack of engagement or your interactive skills (in other words, you're not very fun), then take a look at the *Dog Sports Skills Books* written by me and Deb Jones for detailed help with those issues.

Chapter Ten

Learners and Performers

Some dogs love routine! An obedience dog who will heel for minutes at a time, or perform ten retrieves in a row. An agility dog who will drill contact behaviors or weave poles over and over, showing the same intensity and drive on the last repetition as on the first one. These dogs are performers.

Other dogs enjoy learning and working, but have limited tolerance for repetition. Figuring out a puzzle is a joy for them. They love to master new skills, but hate proofing known behaviors. These dogs are learners.

And of course, some dogs are both; they love both learning and performing! If they are working, they are happy, whether the task at hand is thinking, learning, drilling, or running from one option to the next!

It's worth knowing which your dog prefers so you can structure your training sessions to build on his strengths. To determine if your dog is a learner or a performer, watch your dog. Which causes his tail to wag and his ears to perk up: picking up the clicker for a shaping session or heading into a ring for a formal run through? Does your dog look just as motivated on the fifth repetition as on the first?

Let's look at both types in a bit more detail.

The Learner

The learner loves to use his brain, but once he's learned something, he's ready to move on to something new. These dogs find doing many repetitions to be boring, and may choose to opt out the tenth time you ask him to do the same thing. However, if your dog is opting out of work because he's failing, it's more likely that he's stressed, not bored. In that case, reconsider how you are teaching the exercise and make changes to allow for a lot more success. If he opts out even when he's doing great work, and even when you've got a motivator he loves, he probably is more of a learner.

At first glance, it would appear that the solution is to simply avoid patterns with dogs who lack tolerance for repetition. Perform an exercise once or twice and then move on, focusing on training something new instead. In reality, though, it's not that simple. Repetition is how a learned behavior becomes fluent. And fluency - the stage of training where a dog can perform easily and correctly without conscious thought - is necessary to perform away from home, under stress, and without a cookie in your hand. In other words, fluency is needed for competition.

For learners who need to move from the excitement of a new idea to true fluency, the best approach is to train multiple unrelated pieces of partially known behaviors at the same time.

For example, in one continuous session you might practice a dumbbell hold (three repetitions), pivot on a disc in heel position (three repetitions), a position such as down (three repetitions), and coming into front position (three repetitions). Count out the cookies! There are only three, and when they are gone you must move on to a new bit of behavior. You can cycle through these various bits several times, but by moving from one to the next in quick succession like this, you can prevent the dog from getting bored or frustrated by the sameness of one thing. If you approach it this way, you can still get in as many as nine or twelve repetitions of each of these four behaviors in a single session, but without drilling one option continuously.

Behavior chains are another excellent option because they combine a series of behaviors. For example, instead of working on holding the dumbbell correctly, you would ask for a full retrieve - ONCE. Do not repeat it again, even if your dog got a part wrong. Any dog, regardless of temperament, should work on incorrect links of the chain separate from the whole chain. If your dog is struggling with any particular piece of the exercise, pull that piece out and work with it as suggested above.

Here's what a training session for a learner might look like:

Send your dog to do a formal retrieve over a high jump. If he does it perfectly, move on to three repetitions of nose touches and then three pivots on a disc. Next, you might do a broad jump and then a drop on recall. If you'd like to repeat the formal retrieve over high jump, go ahead, but change it somehow. For example, make your retrieve longer or shorter than your previous throw, or throw your dumbbell into some nearby bushes to give your dog a challenge.

However, let's say you sent your dog to do the retrieve and he failed to do a portion of it correctly - say he went around the jump instead of over it. Now what? Ignore the error! Do three repetitions of the nose touch, three pivots on a disc, and then, instead of trying another retrieve over the high jump, pull out the piece that didn't go so well before. Work on the return only, but only for three repetitions. Then move on to three nose touches, three disc pivots, and THEN try the full retrieve over the high jump.

As you can see, even if your dog cannot handle lots of repetition, there are ways to keep you both happy. Keep the session moving with plenty of variety! This sort of training does take a bit of planning, so make sure that you decide which behaviors you'll work on before you begin your session, and make sure you count out those cookies so you don't get carried away by accident!

The Performer

The performing dog really enjoys knowing what's going to happen in advance. These dogs love to heel for long stretches at a time and are just as happy the tenth time they do something as the first. Dogs who like patterns are often performers - but not always. All dogs want direction and clarity, and for dogs paired with novice trainers who have not yet become good teachers, patterns can be desirable because that's the only time the dog understands what his handler wants from him!

Sometimes performers get a bit stressed when you introduce variations to the basic pattern, or when you try to introduce new behaviors. That's fine. Simply stay at a given point in the learning process a bit longer than you might have otherwise, and use predictable patterns of known behavior as a reward for learning. Work several repetitions of a new behavior and then switch over to a nice, long, relaxing stretch of predictable work; your dog needs that.

Here's what a training session for a performer might look like:

Let's say you're teaching your dog to pivot on a disc. Since performers find learning stressful, do many repetitions before you raise your criteria. You might do ten or more repetitions where you ask your dog to move no more than an inch! Reward that nice effort by stopping there and doing a long stretch of easy and well known work, whether that's heeling for an obedience dog or several runs through a set of weave poles for an agility dog. When you come back to your pivot disc, stay at the same level of effort that your dog gave you last time - only one inch of movement is required to earn a reward - until your dog finds that behavior relatively easy. Even though you might have increased that challenge much quicker with a learner, there's no big hurry to do so with a performer. Go ahead and let your dog settle in to the same work over and over.

Meanwhile, if you want to drill known behaviors like a retrieve over high jump, you'll be able to get away with doing it ten times in a row, and you can take your time adding in proofing elements, because your dog will be thrilled with the repetition. If your dog makes an error and goes around the jump, go ahead and pull out that piece of the exercise. Work on just that part for another ten repetitions or so before going back to the full exercise and see what you have. Feel free to do several repetitions; your dog won't mind.

Keep in Mind...

There is no right or wrong here. Your dog is who he is, and both types of dogs can eventually master all of the skills that you wish to teach. They just have different routes to take them to the same place. Change your strategies according to your dog's preference.

Chapter Eleven

The Ever Changing Dog

 We have spent ten chapters looking at various temperament types and ways to structure your training in order to make your dog stronger. We've talked about building on strengths while respecting weaknesses. And then we've examined how to address those weaknesses just a small bit at a time.

By now, you should know how to create a training plan that accounts for the fact that your dog's core temperament is generally predictable and stable. However, there will always be variables in flux, and you can create a training plan that addresses these variables in order to make your dog stronger and more competent as a learner.

That is what it means to train the dog in front of you. You do not change the temperament that your dog is born with, but you do manipulate your dog's environment, experiences, and training plan to make your dog as strong, responsive, confident, and eager as possible.

No one can account for all of the possible combinations of variables that might come up in competition, but many of them - like the loss of reinforcers, a new environment, and the fact that you are likely to be more nervous - can be predicted and trained for! You can teach your dog that reinforcers still exist, even when they aren't on your body. You can slowly and systematically help your dog learn that new places are safe. You can even train for your own nervousness by videotaping your work (which will make you nervous) or visualizing the ring.

The more you practice all of the possible variables that eventually lead to the dog show picture, the more comfortable your team will be. Train the dog in front of you!

Not ALWAYS...

Although the point of this entire book is to get a feeling for who your dog is, it is also important to recognize that your dog is not ALWAYS "secure" or ALWAYS "cautious." The only thing that you can count on is that all of your dog's qualities will be influenced by many other factors, including the choices you make in training. Consider your dog in as many different lights as possible. Which variables seem to have the greatest influences on your dogs, and which traits are the strongest and most constant regardless of other variables?

Like people, dogs are a complex bundle of possibilities! And while it is likely that his behavior is quite constant, that does not mean that he won't surprise you with a wide range of behaviors, some of which occur very rarely.

Dogs and dog training are not black and white; they are shades of gray because circumstances are ever changing! Recognize that your dog has the capacity for a wide range of behaviors, thoughts, and tendencies, including some that will appear to directly contradict who he is at his core. But even as you recognize this, it's still helpful to understand your dog's general tendencies so you can go out of your way to be conscious of those which appear to cause significant challenges for your dog's training success. Your goal is to maximize the presence of the most desirable package of qualities.

If you pay careful attention, you may find that your dog is actually quite predictable, IF you consider all of the variables that are at play at any given time. One of the best ways to understand your dog and the variables that have been laid out in this book is to look at the instances where you have answered "it depends" and tease apart the variables; what else changed at the same time? That alone may clarify the root issue so that you can create a training plan to address it!

If you really cannot identify any change in any of the variables, the first thing you should consider is that your dog isn't feeling well. Even if he goes to the vet regularly. Even if he has a bevy of specialists. No one can know the feelings that are taking place inside of another, whether physical or mental, because we are not experiencing their feelings. We are simply making educated guesses, and even the most thorough veterinary visit in the world is not going to reveal that your dog has chronic migraine headaches, the beginnings of cancer, or suffers from depression. The realities of pain and illness are often not knowable.

It's also worth considering if something has changed and you're simply not seeing it. Try this experiment: For seven days in a row, train your dog in the same location, at the same time of day, using the same motivator (type and quantity!), for the same length of time, and hold everything possible constant. Obviously, there's no way to be perfectly identical, but do your best. Now, write down your daily results. What do you see? You might find that your dog is quite consistent indeed.

Just like dogs, humans also change over time, but normally we can find the reasons if we really take some time to think through the variables We may like to eat cake, but not if we're sick, distracted, full, tired, excited about guests, stressed about losing a job, worried about our spouse, or…the possibilities are endless, really. We might always say, "I like cake," when asked, but we also recognize that at any given moment, our behavior might belie that fact.

When using this book, your job is to ferret out what qualities you consider to be stable and defining characteristics ("I like cake!") and from there, identify which variables might change our expression of that interest ("…but not when I'm exhausted!").

Your dog likes to work! But maybe not when tired, stressed, worried, or placed in a novel situation.

If you've read this far, I hope you're developing some thoughts about who you think your dog is. Now, go back through the chapters and identify where you are facing your biggest challenges and work on them. But remember, behavior issues must always be addressed first! If you think your dog is scared or nervous, forget training and work through that basic issue first - only train actual skills when you're in places where your dog is comfortable and secure.

Chapter Twelve

The Dog-Handler Match

 We don't always get what we want or need - or what we thought we wanted or needed. We've all heard about the novice handler who has never owned a dog before, but decides to get a working line German Shepherd Dog, dead set on learning the protection sports as a fun hobby to fill their spare time. Even though it often ends poorly, there is nothing wrong with the dog, nor is there anything wrong with the handler. But there is definitely a mismatch between what the dog is capable of and the handler's training experience and sophistication.

The reverse also occurs; a highly sophisticated trainer does her research and purchases the "right" puppy – who grows up into the wrong adult. The trainer wanted a Ferrari but got a Toyota.

What Do You Want In A Dog?

People tend to like certain kinds of dogs - dogs who mesh well with their style. People who like rules and who are more orderly in their training tend to like stronger, sturdier dogs. Softer people may prefer more fragile dogs who can be given a lot of choice. Some people like to be more directive and controlling with their animals and need a dog who can live under that. And of course, some people really haven't got a clue – they just want a dog and acquire one with no thought at all. It's something to think about when you get a dog - does this dog match your style?

If you're reading this book, you probably already have a dog. So the question becomes: did you get the dog you were hoping for? Or are you disappointed in some aspects of your dog? Or worse, are you resentful that you didn't get the dog that you thought you were getting? It can be a bitter pill to swallow if you had visions of one dog and the dog in front of you is completely different. The fact is, not all dogs are cut out for all dog sports, no matter how hard you work. Indeed, some dogs are truly not cut out for any dog sports!

Before you throw in the towel, ask yourself if you are being realistic about the inherent tradeoffs that come with different packages of temperament. For example, do you expect your dog to be super calm and self sufficient in the house and yet high drive and handler focused for training? Although those dogs exist, they're not common.

Take the time to find the points where you and your dog mesh particularly well. Then, when you are frustrated over the areas where your temperaments clash, remember the good and try to stay positive.

What Does Your Dog Want In A Human?

What do you think your dog would like to have in a human partner? Let's anthropomorphize for a moment and consider training and human interaction from the dog's point of view.

Dogs tend to gravitate towards certain kinds of trainers - people who mesh well with their style. Dogs who like rules and clarity tend to like humans who are clear, directive, and goal oriented in their training. Softer dogs need softer humans who give them plenty of choices and time to settle into their training with no particular set of goals on the horizon. Some dogs seem to thrive on a more controlling human. Others have an independent spirit and seem to resist almost any efforts to redirect them to the human's interests.

Are you are the human your dog hoped for? Do you think your dog is happy with you as a trainer? Do you have a naturally good fit with your dog, or is it something that you'll have to be mindful of in order to bring out the best in your dog?

No doubt if dogs were aware of the choices, they would all choose a trainer who understood excellent training, was sensitive to their body language and any emotional distress, attended to their physical and emotional needs, avoided angry and confusing outbursts, and was kind, clear, and compassionate as a trainer. The fact is, excellent training is excellent training, and all dogs thrive on excellent training. Still, dogs, like people, also come with very individual personalities. Some dogs would hope for the lap of luxury as a pampered pet and others would pine for the thrill of competition and the chance to use every fiber of their brains and bodies. Most fall in between. Although trainers who can meet all of the needs of their dogs do exist, they are not common.

How Can You Work Together?

As you look back over what you want in your dog, and as you then consider what your dog most likely wants from you, it should be obvious that neither side of the equation is going to get exactly what they wanted.

Perfection does not exist, so we all have to give. Your dog gives to you because he has no choice; he lives in your house and is directed by your decisions. And you give because your dog comes with a package of characteristics and experiences that you did not necessarily choose, but you still have to live with.

It is an utter waste of time and energy to worry about every second of your training, every mistake you have made, every moment that you made a good or a poor decision. Your dog will adapt to you because that is what dogs do. What we can do is empathize with them to the best of our ability and remain cognizant of the fact that our dogs really have limited choices in their lives – we chose them and they did not choose us. They got the trainer that you are today, whether sophisticated and aware or bumbling and oblivious.

Rules of Thumb

As you strive to be the best possible trainer for your dog, keep these things in mind:

If your dog is expressing emotional distress, something is wrong with your training or the environment. Always. Remember that fear trumps all. If your dog's behavior is fearful, you must address that before adding anything else – even free cookies. If your dog feels safe and secure, then engagement can follow, but not before.

If your dog is expressing notable frustration behaviors, something is wrong with your training. Always. While some dogs have more tolerance for ambiguity than others, the fact is that great trainers are unlikely to see frustration in their dogs because they set up their sessions for success, keep their rates of reinforcement extremely high, and have mastered the basics of training. If you're seeing frustration, stop! Re-read the relevant portions of this book. Learn all you can about excellent, clean training. And then try again.

If your dog is disengaged and you are still training, then something is wrong with your training. Always. You must not train a disengaged dog! While dogs, like people, can become bored with any given activity, a well-structured training program respects the needs of the dog and evaluates the dog's level of engagement continuously over the minutes, days, and months of your work together. Never train a disengaged dog. Stop and reconsider how you wish to proceed.

If you learn nothing else from this book, learn to pay attention. Always. What is your dog's body language, behavior, and level of engagement telling you? Keep those firmly on the positive side of the scale and you will be the best trainer that you can be for your dog, regardless of your technical skills at any point in time.

If you follow these rules of thumb, will you reach success? Probably, but not always.

Worst Case Scenarios

You had a plan. After doing a good deal of research, you picked your breed and your breeder with care. You received your puppy; you were so excited! You might have had some niggling doubts initially, but you pushed that aside - he's perfect! And he will be your companion in life and in dog sports for the foreseeable future.

Then you started to notice things. Maybe he seemed prone to injury. At first you thought it was normal puppy growing pains, but soon it led to a series of vet appointments. Maybe he seemed uncomfortable with new people, and not just a little uncomfortable, but distressed to the point that he was growling and lunging at strangers. Maybe in new places he panicked and soon he didn't want to get in or out of the car. Maybe he screamed and barked each time you tried to crate him and leave your house, to the point where your neighbors were calling the police.

By the time your promising puppy made it to adulthood, your hopes were dashed. Maybe your breeder, friends, or family were full of helpful advice, but no one seemed to understand how bad the situation really was. Or maybe they were blaming you for everything that was going wrong. Regardless, you feel terrible. This is not what you had planned.

If the issues are behavioral, you might be angry or frustrated at the dog. If he would just trust you, he'd see that people are fine. If he'd just relax and look around when you went somewhere new, he'd see that panicking in new environments is stupid. If he'd chew his toy in his crate, he'd realize that being left alone is no big deal!

If the issues are physical, you might also be angry or frustrated, even though you know it's not his fault. He doesn't want to be injured either! But you're not thinking rationally anymore. You're just tired of it. You're tired of missing training, you're tired of going to the vet, and you're tired of paying the bills.

Rationally, you know that life isn't fair, but your emotions aren't following suit. Unfortunately, your dog can no more help who he is than you can help how you feel about who he is. He's just a dog with behaviors and a physical constitution that are a combination of his genetics and his life experiences. And you're just a human with emotions that happen spontaneously.

Both of you have the same problem, but not from the same perspective. What you have in common is unhappiness.

You cannot control your emotions, but you can control your behavior. As the human, you get to make the hard choices about what to do now. Do you have the time and the emotional or financial resources to work through your dog's issues? Are the issues even fixable? How is your dog's quality of life? How is your quality of life? Does the pursuit of dog sports, with this dog, really make any sense for the two of you? Might your dog be better off in a new home, without the pressure of disappointment and unhappiness hanging in the air between the two of you? Consider your options with care.

No one gets exactly what they were looking for. Fortunately, most of us end up with much more modest issues to work through, but there are no perfect dogs. If your dog's worst behavior is running out of the ring to greet his friends, take a moment to be thankful; others are experiencing much more troubling scenarios.

Nature vs. Nurture

I am often asked if there is a way to test a young puppy in order to identify the basic temperament qualities discussed. This question is hard to answer; by the time I see a puppy turn into an adult, I am also seeing the effects of all of the training and life experiences that the dog has had. If the owner has worked hard to develop the dog's suitability for dog sports, then the dog's temperament developed as a result of both genetics and handler effort.

I believe that many qualities are innate. Dogs are born with a basic temperament; the same as people! I can easily look at the similarities in littermates (and to some extent, in breeds and lines) to come to this conclusion. But we humans heavily influence the end result. No doubt about that either.

This book was written to help you understand who your dog is right now so that you can structure your training appropriately. This will allow you to bring out the best in your dog over time.

If your dog is handler sensitive, you can structure training sessions that allow your dog to be right A LOT, and that will reduce your dog's sensitivity. If your dog has low working drive, then you can increase it by making training as fun as possible, keeping sessions short, and not trialing more than your dog can enjoy. If your dog is super sensitive to you, be particularly aware of your expressions and visible emotions - forever! And watch your dog become sturdier as a result of lots of success.

If you are working with your wallflower and suddenly the dog makes a bold move - celebrate! Even if that bold move involved stealing a cookie out of your hand! When your environmental dog checks in - celebrate! Even when there is nothing out there that you can even identify as a potential issue. When your nervous Nelly goes more than 20 feet away from you, curious to check stuff out - celebrate! Oh, and quit with the impulse control games with your dog who never showed any interest in getting out of the crate in the first place; you don't need that!

Take the time to recognize what is right with your dog. Notice how her unique package of traits make her extra special, and the ways in which they make her easier to train. Some handlers will have to work harder to bring out their dog's best "package" than others, and in some cases, the dog will never achieve the goals the handler had set. Work towards what you can influence, gently and steadily. Accept what you cannot influence and then identify the positives in those qualities - so that you can love your dog in spite of her flaws.

Your dog is doing her best. She puts up with you and where you are in your training journey; work to give her the same benefit. If you find ways to focus on the process - where you have come from and where you are going - you will enjoy your dog a good deal more than if you focus on goals, some of which may not be realistic or attainable for your team at all. It's not relevant what your friend's dog is achieving; your friend does not have your dog, and your dog does not have her for a trainer. Your dog has you. You have him. And that's just fine.

Postscript

This was the most difficult book I've ever written. Indeed, on several occasions I almost gave up altogether, yet time after time, I found myself pulled back to my computer, determined to try again.

I was incredibly frustrated trying to find a clear and logical order in which to lay out the topics. The concepts described here are so completely interwoven with one another that figuring out where one started and the other ended felt close to insurmountable, yet undeniably important. How can one understand power dynamics without understanding self-control? How can one understand self-control without understanding working drive? And why are we talking about power dynamics, self-control or working drive at all, when stress is so often the underlying driver of problematic behavior?

Then I thought I should start with issues of temperament. Is your dog secure or cautious? Is he high drive or low drive? But that's not obvious either, because powerful and driven dogs focused on food or toys may appear very secure, even when they are not. So if you think your dog is secure, driven, and impulsive but really you've got a power dynamics problem…

And I'm quite sure that I have left important pieces out! Surely I could have offered different ways of looking at this topic, with different combinations, orders, examples, or considerations. Indeed, maybe I should have simply presented case study after case study, considering each dog on his own merits.

So what was it about this book that kept me in the game? Why bother at all considering I was often moderately distressed by the entire project?

Simply put, I believe this topic defines me as a trainer. I always begin training with a hard look at the dog in front of me. Indeed, this quality is so powerful within me that I cannot prevent it; I see the dog in front of me, even when I would rather not. I see the fear, the subtle signs of avoidance, and the worried interactions with the handler, and I want to make things better. Not just for the dog, but for the trainer too! I also see the enthusiastic dogs with bright eyes and a willing heart and I see the smiles and joy that this creates for both parts of the team. I want to see more of that in all of dog training! What qualities of this dog are driving this dog's behavior at this moment in time? That is the question that leads us to the answer.

Ultimately, I wrote this book because I want to share my passion for seeing a dog for who he really is.

What should a writer do when she wishes to communicate about an incredibly complex and important topic, even when the topic seems to run in circles? Does she walk away from the project altogether or simply jump in and persist?

That depends on the qualities of the human. This human, the one writing this book? Well, she has compulsive tendencies that don't allow her to give up easily, but with a contradictory serving of both self-control and impulsiveness. She is secure in temperament, generally stable, and with a tendency to move more and exhibit frantic behavior under stress. She is highly motivated by writing, studying complex dogs, and she thrives on learning. She is a bundle of apparent contradictions - until you take a little time to ferret out the relevant variables, and to recognize the interplay between her genetic tendencies and her modifying life experiences. Then it all makes sense.

So what, then, is this human likely to do when faced with a challenging topic; a book that she desperately wants to write, but which frustrates her at every turn? Is she likely to jump in and keep writing or walk away? Well, clearly, she will jump in and keep writing!

Forgive me where this book feels jumbled, confused, incomplete, or simply overwhelming. I've done my best for you because this topic is my passion; watching dogs, trying to understand them, loving them, and training them to the best of our abilities.

Forgive me, too, where it seems like I'm pushing my other books. Because issues of temperament, behavior, training, and emotions are so thoroughly intertwined, I struggled to encapsulate the full complexity of the topic in a single book. Many of the issues presented in this book are equally complex, and while I could have written deeper explanations for tackling those issues, it was beyond the scope of this book to do so. Further, I have already written at length about those very issues in my other books, and so I have referred the reader to them.

With all of that said, I am going to suggest that you read this book more than one time.

First, go through this book as a "reading" book. Try to wrap your head around the concepts; "feel" the extent to which these ideas are totally intertwined with each other. Recognize and appreciate just how complex behavior and excellent training really is!

Next, read for a holistic understanding, starting with your own dog. Where does your dog fall on the spectrum of each trait presented? Which ones make you respond, "Well, it depends..." As you read it this second time, my references to other chapters will begin to resonate in your head, and you'll start to get a feel for the whole. Can you begin to guess what I might say next?

Finally, see if you can begin to see patterns in other dogs. Are you getting faster? Do you find yourself making predictions about dogs based on very limited information, based on what you can see? Can you articulate where your guesses came from? The day people ask you if you are a mind reader is the day you know you're on your way.

Remember, when it comes to the complex interplay of temperament and behavior, there is no starting point, and there is no ending point. There is simply a growing understanding as you absorb how the interwoven pieces affect each other. Further, no aspect of dog behavior exists in a vacuum. You have to understand all of the pieces both together and separately before you can stand back and begin to recognize the unique tapestry that represents who your dog really is. And from this point of understanding, you will begin to find a training plan that is most logical for your specific situation.

Enjoy the journey.